The Little Water
Medicine Society
of the Senecas

The council of animal familiars restores the life of Good Hunter. Watercolor by Sanford Plumber (Seneca). Courtesy of the Buffalo (New York) Museum of Science.

The Little Water Medicine Society of the Senecas

William N. Fenton

University of Oklahoma Press
Norman

ALSO BY WILLIAM N. FENTON

Songs from the Iroquois Longhouse (Washington, D.C., 1942)
(ed.) *Symposium on Local Diversity in Iroquois Culture* (Washington, D.C., 1951)
The Iroquois Eagle Dance: An Offshoot of the Calumet Dance (Washington, D.C., 1953)
American Indian and White Relations to 1830 (Chapel Hill, 1957)
(co-ed.) *Symposium on Cherokee and Iroquois Culture* (Washington, D.C., 1961)
(ed.) *Parker on the Iroquois* (Syracuse, N.Y. 1968)
(ed. and trans., with E. L. Moore) *Customs of the American Indians, Compared with the Customs of Primitive Times, by Father Joseph-Francois Lafitau*, two vols. (Toronto, 1974–76)
The False Faces of the Iroquois (Norman, 1987)
The Great Law and the Longhouse: A Political History of the Iroquois Confederacy (Norman, 1998)

This book is published with the generous assistance of The McCasland Foundation, Duncan, Oklahoma.

LIBRARY OF CONGRESS CATALOGING-IN-PUBLICATION DATA

Fenton, William Nelson, 1908–
    The Little Water Medicine Society of the Senecas / William N. Fenton.
        p. cm.—(The civilization of the American Indian series; v. 242)
    Includes bibliographical references and index.
    ISBN 0-8061-3447-X (hc: alk. paper)
        1. Little Water Medicine Society—History. 2. Seneca Indians—Rites and cere-
monies. 3. Seneca Indians—Medicine. 4. Seneca Indians—Religion. 5. Medicine
bundles—Allegheny River Valley (Pa. and N.Y.) 6. Allegheny River Valley (Pa. and
N.Y.)—Social life and customs. I. Title. II. Series
E99.S3F46 2002
974.7004'9755–dc21   2002018875

The *Little Water Medicine Society of the Senecas* is Volume 242 in The Civilization of the American Indian Series.

The paper in this book meets the guidelines for permanence and durability of the Committee on Production Guidelines for Book Longevity of the Council on Library Resources, Inc. ∞

1   2   3   4   5   6   7   8   9   10

Contents

Illustrations

Introduction

Although the League of the Five Nations and the False Face Society may be the two most famous features of Iroquois life (Fenton 1987, 1998), traditionalists regard the Little Water Medicine Society, with its ceremonies for renewing the strength of its medicine bundles and for celebrating cures, as crucial to maintaining their way of life. Yet the nature and activities of the society remain known little to science and not at all to the public.

Residents of Salamanca, New York, a thriving city of some ten thousand in the 1920s situated on land leased from the Seneca Nation, had known Indians all of their lives but had no idea what went on downriver on the reservation. In the summer of 1933, during my first fieldwork on the Allegany Reservation, I called on a former college classmate in Salamanca whose family were leading citizens, although by then the Great Depression had reduced their business. A partner in the firm, who had competed in sports with and against Indians and who regularly frequented the mouth of Coldspring Creek fishing for brown trout, asked me, "What are all those Indians doing walking the roads at night carrying pails and bundles?" At the time I didn't know, but I would soon find out.

That summer I pitched my tent on "Snow Street" in the dooryard of Jonas Snow, who accepted me as a guest. Jonas carved masks for my father and referred to him as the "old man," and Jonas's father, Amos, and my father's father had been "friends," in the Iroquois sense. I shared meals with the Snow family—Josephine (not the greatest cook), Windsor, Linus, Bemis, and Theresa—and after supper we shared Arthur Parker's photographs of his sources at Cattaraugus in books I had brought with me. Jonas knew many of the principals, whom he identified, and he volunteered bits about their roles in the medicine societies. He not only answered my queries but, as the occasion arose, mentioned his own participation in the medicine society—properly, the Little Water Medicine Society. A casual visitor on Snow Street who later proved to be son of the principal bundle keeper cautioned me with tales of the power of the medicine.

When work with the "regular gang" of Erie Railroad track workers filled Jonas's days, I turned to another of my father's mask sources, Chauncey Johnny John, with whom I began a collaboration that lasted until his death in the 1950s. We began by collecting specimens of herbal medicines in the fields and wooded hillsides of the Allegheny Valley, which I arranged to have identified by botanists at a nearby field station. We actually discovered several species previously unknown to them. But of greater interest to us just then were occasions when Chauncey named the odd plant as an ingredient of "the medicine." Years later, Chauncey honored my interest by tutoring me in the lore and ceremonies of the Little Water Society.

Henry Redeye, with his son Sherman and daughter-in-law Clara, hosted me during the midwinter ceremonies, and I lived with them a second summer, which enabled me to make systematic inquiries about the medicine societies and their rituals. Both for my benefit and to discharge their personal obligations, they hung the kettle (sponsored feasts) for several orders of the curing celebration rite, *i:ʔdo:s,*[1] so that I could observe the elaboration of ritual patterns in actual performance. John Jimerson of High Bank, then the dominant

---

1. The colon in Seneca words denotes increased vowel length. The raised "question mark without the period" is a glottal stop, an essential consonant in Iroquoian languages.

figure at such feasts, having first spoken against my research in the longhouse, ultimately accepted me as a pupil and proved himself an excellent teacher.

For important cultural activities, the Iroquois appeal to origin legends that describe the purpose and content of the activity that a person or group is expected to discharge. The legend of the Good Hunter who is resuscitated by the medicine animals in a rite called *i:ʔdo:s* or *hadi:ʔdo:s* affords the rationale for celebrating that cure by persons who themselves have received "the great good medicine" or who have dreamed about its rites or paraphernalia. Two of my living sources knew the Good Hunter legend but failed to mention a second legend describing the search for the plant medicine; this second one was known to previous generations of Senecas at Cattaraugus, the other reservation of the Seneca Nation of Indians (Parker 1908: 153–56). The story about the search for the plant medicine underpins the society's ceremony to renew the medicine (*hadiyenʔgwaʔye:ni*).

Accordingly, the Little Water medicine is of two kinds—an older, original medicine made from the thighs, hearts, and brains of mammals and birds who joined in compounding a powder for reviving Good Hunter, and a second, more recent plant medicine derived from a bleeding cornstalk and a squash that are believed to grow on a remote mountain. The plant variety includes, besides, some twelve to twenty herbals. The "night song," *gano:daʔ,* ascribed to Whippoorwill, guided two fasting hunters to surmount a series of obstacles to reach its source. There they hacked the cornstalk, which bled and regenerated itself. They also brought away squash for rattles to prop up the song. Of the alleged plant ingredients, only saxifrage figures in the songs of the renewal. The original meat medicine has long since been used up, and no person now living knows how to replenish either kind.

The medicine has relieved concussions, reduced fractures, and healed wounds—reportedly including gunshot wounds. Indeed, historically it comes down from bundles that Seneca war parties carried during the eighteenth century. Its rituals resemble those reported for shamanistic societies from seventeenth-century Huronia. Holding a bundle is an awesome responsibility. The possibility of witchcraft by a malicious bundle holder lurks as a pervasive fear in the community. Although individuals hold bundles, the medicine is regarded as community or tribal property. In general, participation in its rites is restricted to society members, although "secrecy," as reported by Arthur C. Parker (1909), was more prevalent in the first decade of the twentieth century. Admission to the society's rites relaxed in later decades.

The Little Water Society comprises both the bundle holders (*honontcinohgen?*) and persons they have treated with any form of their ceremony. Or one may dream of the ceremony or any of its paraphernalia. Clairvoyants play a significant role in interpreting dreams by water scrying to divine what form of ceremony the person should sponsor. A person may also discharge an inherited obligation to fulfill one of the medicine's several rites by hanging a kettle and setting down a feast for the society. Membership thus includes patients, dreamers, and inheritors.

Readers may wonder why these elaborate ceremonies continue to be performed. Maintaining Iroquois ceremonial culture requires constant renewal, and individuals who adhere to the old ways feel compelled to renew their obligations to ceremonies that have helped them. This sense that one must renew one's ceremonies is what keeps the culture going. Keepers of major rituals may feel that they have been chosen by the ceremony to perform certain roles in maintaining that rite. These points are important in understanding what follows.

Twice a year, and sometimes three times, the medicine society meets to sing for the medicine and renew its potency: regularly in the fall, when the animals renew their coats for winter, and in the spring, when the animals shed their winter coats for summer, and sometimes at midwinter, if the society has treated someone between sessions. The fall meeting calls for singing all four periods, or groups of songs, of the renewal rite, which comprises some ninety-six songs. The songs of Period I recount the quest for the plant medicine; those of Period II announce the arrival of various animals bringing tobacco;

Period III acknowledges the wounded culture hero, Good Hunter; and in Period IV, various waterfowl surface until Raven wheels in flight and settles down midfield, ending the cycle. Only the autumn sing calls for all four periods; otherwise the singers omit the third period. The renewal ceremony takes its name, *hadiyen?gwa?ye:ni hadino:daiyai?*, "the songs for spreading, or putting down, tobacco," from each participant's bringing a packet of tobacco, which is contributed to the invocation. The name may also derive from the fact that the headman, or conductor (at Tonawanda), puts down eight pinches of tobacco and picks them up at the end of the ceremony.

No theme in Iroquois culture history has greater force than the belief in the power of song. The songs for administering the Little Water medicine and then releasing it after the patient has been confined for four days pertain to the celebration rite known as *i:?do:s*, which is the vehicle through which individuals discharge their obligation to renew a cure by the medicine or to fulfill a dream of some aspect of the ceremony. *I:?do:s* is the celebration of membership in the medicine company, but it has an integrity of its own. Persons may be helped by any form of its ceremonies without recourse to the medicine itself.

The medicine company, or society, is indeed a shamanistic society, and aspects of shamanism permeate its ceremonies. A respected source suggested that the term *hadi:?do:s*, "they are performing it," refers to boiling something, possibly the songs (*gahi:?dohon*), which recalls the widespread stunt of shamans plunging their arms into boiling kettles. Songs allude to sweat-house activities such as juggling hot rocks, to traipsing a patient through fires the length of the house, and to threats to burn another's bed.

Seneca medicine society rites conform to a pattern that I previously established for the Eagle Dance (Fenton 1953): announcements, a tobacco invocation, the ritual proper, thanking participants, and a terminal feast. The renewal ceremony for the medicine and the several orders of celebration rites adhere to this common Iroquois feast pattern.

In typical Iroquois fashion, the rites of the medicine company feature separation into moieties. The four clans of the moiety opposite that of the patient or sponsor assume the major roles in conducting and performing the ceremony. Reciprocally, the four clans of the host's moiety organize the feast and respond to speeches and songs, and at the end their speaker thanks the participants of both sides for their services. Each side appoints messengers and conductors to manage the ceremony. The two sides sit facing each other across the "fire." They make reciprocal speeches and throw songs across the fire, the visitors invariably acting first, and the hosts replying. The conductor of each side has a bag of rattles, which he dumps on the floor together with the songs. And midway through the ceremony, the two sides reciprocate in the curing songs, when the two conductors alternately shuttle the patient the length of the house beside the fire. Finally, the visiting moiety enlists a masker who marshals the great round dance and blows ashes on the host.

The music of the all-night ceremony to renew the medicine has a singularly beautiful quality that is appreciated by participants and other Senecas as well. Nonparticipating members of the society may bring tobacco and sit in an outer room of the lodge, while others are free to listen outside. The late Nick Bailey of Tonawanda, himself an accomplished musician and flautist with major orchestras, favored listening to the singers from the road outside the lodge to sitting in their midst, and he rarely missed a session. As an outsider who became an insider, I concede that Nick had a point.

Edmund Wilson, whom I introduced to the society at Tonawanda and who sat with me among the singers, captured the essence of the renewal ceremony for American letters (Wilson 1959; see also Fenton 1991.) At the time, he told the society that he was a writer and that he might say something about the experience, and no one objected, despite the brouhaha generated later by a person who claimed a proprietary right to speak for the Senecas after Wilson's account appeared in *The New Yorker*. Just then I was blamed for it, although within a year Chief Corbett Sundown, our host at the time, visited the state museum in Albany and, as he departed, turned to me and said, "We are having it next week. You had better come." Unfortunately, official business intervened. Indeed, the Senecas are a forgiving people.

Readers may wonder how I became involved in affairs of the Little Water Society and how I gathered information on its lore and ceremonies. I set out in my research to establish the relationship of the ceremony to renew the Little Water medicine (*hadiyen?gwa?ye:ni*) to the rites known collectively as *i:?do:s,* by which individuals celebrate adherence to the medicine company. The structure of the medicine society, or society of shamans, and the order of ceremonies they perform emerged for me only gradually in the course of my study. I kept a journal of incidental topics—things told to me in passing, happenings that I attended and observed when I could not take notes. The journal was crucial in my early years of fieldwork, when everything had equal importance. Field notes of a more systematic nature filled notebooks that I numbered by source, place, and time; these are now archived in the Fenton Collection in the library of the American Philosophical Society in Philadelphia.

At midwinter 1934, the husband of the matron of my adoptive clan—also sister to my sponsor, Jonas Snow—gave me a systematic account of the renewal ceremony, as a participant, and recommended that I attend the next time they met. During the 1930s and 1940s, whenever I was near Coldspring, on the Allegany Reservation, I seldom missed a session to renew the medicine. I sat with the singers and began to learn what to expect. For two and a half years (1935–37), while I was resident at Tonawanda for the U.S. Indian Service, the local society opened its lodge to me, affording a comparison with Coldspring and with Newtown, which is on the Cattaraugus Reservation. Jesse Cornplanter, disturbed by local variants at Tonawanda, accompanied me to his native Newtown, where he persuaded principals of the medicine company there to clarify my understanding of the relationship between the Little Water and *i:?do:s.* I then went back to Allegany, where Sherman Redeye and Chauncey Johnny John classified the varieties of *i:?do:s* performed locally. These understandings prepared me in the 1940s to hear Jesse Cornplanter dictate from Arthur Parker's field notes the Edward

Cornplanter version of *i:ʔdo:s,* which Jesse, Edward's son, regarded as authentic. And Parker provided me with photostatic copies of his free translation of the *i:ʔdo:s* song cycle from around 1907.

The advent of electronic recorders, first using aluminum disks, then acetate, and later tapes, in the late 1930s and early 1940s enabled me to record the *i:ʔdo:s* cycle from the Onondaga chief Joseph Logan at Six Nations Reserve in 1941 (Fenton 1942a, 1942b; and see Appendix C), and within a month Chauncey and Richard Johnny John at Coldspring recorded the Seneca version. Whenever possible I wrote out the song texts in field notebooks and went over them afterward with the singers, because early on George Herzog cautioned me that song texts accommodated spoken text to the melodic line, and notebooks captured informant remarks about the text that escaped electronic recordings. In stage two, I typed up my field notes. The original disks are deposited in the Library of Congress; copies went to Gertrude Kurath, who, working from my stage two field notes, transcribed the music and described the dances (Kurath 1964; and see Appendix B).

After the midwinter ceremonies of 1941, when I had again sat with the singers to renew the medicine, Chauncey remarked that I knew some of it, and it was time I learned it all. He consented to record the four periods for my instruction, although he was not in the best of voice, and we made a tape from duplicate disks. The Library of Congress holds the originals, and from the first tape, now in the Fenton Collection at the American Philosophical Society, I held a duplicate for study.

Recently, I answered an appeal from the late James Skye of Six Nations explaining that his people no longer could sing for the medicine and asking whether I had a tape of the Seneca version from Coldspring Longhouse, which they regarded as authentic. I sent the tape, the Six Nations singers recovered the songs, and Jim put the tape on his kitchen shelf, from which it vanished before he could mail it.

My stage two write-up of the Johnny John version of *i:ʔdo:s* had a different fate. I sent a carbon copy to Dick Johnny John, which he

used as a guide for another scholar—a poet who produced a remarkable literary piece (Rothenberg 1972).

Ethnology is a learning process, and inevitably later observations
reflect previous understandings of how participants saw things. My
practice has been to seek out the pattern of sequence that Iroquois
people follow in performing each of their ceremonies, and of which
they are often unconscious, and once I discover this paradigm, to
organize my materials accordingly. When the pattern is brought to
their attention, sources say: "This is what we always do." Patterns
governing major ceremonies such as the calendrical festivals may be
more explicit, and sources tick them off quite consciously. I ask my
sources to describe the ceremonies in their own terms; I then
observe ritual behavior (what they actually do) and ask my sources to
point out what is important to them. We later fill in the longer
parts—speeches, ritual song texts, recordings, and so forth. My collaborators have more than once staged performances "just so I could
see it."

This book both orders the structure of the ceremonies as they are
performed and mirrors my learning about them. It is presented
largely in the form of my notes from the time, which I have edited
only lightly. Readers will find much in the form of lists and outlines,
and I beg their patience with a certain amount of repetition, loose-
ness of organization, and variation in spellings of Seneca words.
Considered as primary documents, these chapters will, I hope, bring
to the Little Water Medicine Society the public understanding it
deserves. And may the record of what I learned help the present generation of Senecas to revive any parts they have lost.

The Little Water
Medicine Society
of the Senecas

◆ I ◆

"They Who Carry Pails by Night…"

The Little Water Society assumed a preeminent place among a dozen medicine societies that the Senecas of western New York celebrated in the 1930s and 1940s, followed by the closely associated Eagle Dance; both were originally associated with warfare. The Little Water medicine, which the Senecas call, phonemically, *niga:negaʔa:h dwahso:t,* "a little water, our grandparent," other Iroquois refer to as *gano:daʔ,* after the song and the sound of the flute. The medicine society, its rituals and cures, and its rules for membership have been known to the literature of anthropology and folklore for a century. Arthur C. Parker (1908, 1909) first brought it to scientific notice; Edmund Wilson (1959) claimed it for American letters; and I described it for the annals of medicine (Fenton 1979). Yet the whole subject is poorly understood. Until now, there has been no monograph on the subject, and it remains an avowed (and, paradoxically, much talked about) secret among the Iroquois today.

Traditional Longhouse-religion adherents and progressive Christians alike have sought the society's cures, although it is traditionalists who guard the medicine and keep up the ceremonies to renew it. Occasionally, white friends have been admitted to the renewal ceremony to hear the songs and have been asked to contribute to the feast, and several non-Iroquois people have held packets of the medicine. Personally, I have never wanted to possess any of the medicine, nor have I ever sought to collect it for a museum. But I have repeatedly attended the ceremonies to renew the medicine, I have listened when its keepers volunteered to explain its mysteries, I have been instructed by the principal song holders, and I have taken texts and recorded the songs for posterity. In recent years I have made these recordings available to native singers. No one ever told me that I might not understand the mysteries of the Little Water medicine, and I never pledged not to recall or write about them. Such matters are sacred to believers, who may be disturbed to see them in print, but the materials in two boxes of my field notes cry out for release, explanation, and synthesis.

Although some Iroquois feel strongly about the subject, many of them have no knowledge of the Little Water medicine, never having attended any of its rites. They share this ignorance with educated neighbors. The curious person living in a community adjacent to the reservation inquires of the visiting anthropologist, "What are all those Indians doing who walk the roads at night carrying pails and bundles?" An adequate answer, based on a lifetime of looking, asking, and listening to the old people, requires a book. I did once publish a summary report on what the medicine is, in which I described the obligations of bundle holders, abstracted the origin myth, and sketched the ritual pattern for renewing the medicine (Fenton 1979). I mentioned the rituals of curing, of releasing the medicine, and of celebrating individual cures. I now expand that treatment to encompass the available data.

Two Kinds of Medicine

Living with a Seneca family, one soon learns that there is a sovereign remedy that comes into use when someone cuts his foot, when a lacrosse player suffers a broken bone, when a baseball player is hit with a pitched ball or when a foul ball strikes a spectator, when a person is knocked on the head and loses consciousness, or when someone is the victim of an automobile accident. In such cases Senecas rely on the "great good medicine," also known as "small dose" or "little water." This famous medicine is of two kinds. The older and more powerful is a powder composed of the dried hearts and pectoral muscles of game animals and predators. This compound once constituted the tribal war bundle, but it is now in scarce supply. The little that remains today is guarded carefully and used sparingly.

The second kind comprises the powders of fourteen to twenty plant species that are confined to a few places in the swamps and on the hills of the Allegheny country in southwestern New York. It includes a species of "wild cornstalk" and a squash; these two reveal themselves only to the most dedicated plant hunter, who must first seclude himself, refrain from sexual activity, fast, and purify himself. He must also be a person who has violated none of the principles of nature. Since these conditions are impossible to meet in contemporary American Indian society, the plant variety has become nearly as scarce as the animal kind. A few herbalists claim to know which plants are in it, but I never succeeded in obtaining a consistent list of ingredients. No two lists are identical, nor are they complete. Possibly my sources withheld one or two last ingredients necessary to complete the formula. However, I am inclined to think that the herbalists whom I consulted simply did not know quite all of the ingredients.

The secret formula for mixing the plant medicine is alleged to have died with John Patterson of Cattaraugus Reservation in the last century; people say that his bundle was the source of the medicine remaining among the Seneca Nation (Parker 1908: 163). The lists of roots that made up its contents are at best sophisticated guesses.

Agreement centers, however, on two mythical plants that are most difficult to find: wild cornstalk and wild squash. Wild cornstalk is commonly thought to grow in the deep woods on a high mountain. The stalk resembles a tree trunk, and from it issues the song of the medicine, accompanied by the rattle of the squash, which grows beside it. Cornstalk bleeds when cut into, but it has power to regenerate itself. The man who first followed the song to its source, discovered the cornstalk, and took a piece of its root, which extends in the cardinal directions, noticed that it bled like a living wound when he chopped into it. He dried and mixed these two plants together. I found no agreement on the remaining twelve to eighteen plant species that make up the powder.

The original and more powerful medicine is composed of the hearts and muscles of carnivorous animals and predatory birds and the brains of several small birds. Again the lists differ. And the actors in the origin myth assume different roles and have different names in the several versions. They include an extinct fauna comprising mythical giant progenitors of later animals known to the Senecas: Flying Lion (a meteor), Naked Bear, Beaver, Mink, and Panther. Among the principal giant birds of the firmament are Dew Eagle, a great duck, and particularly *gahga?go:wa:*, the giant crow or Raven, who as leader and messenger of the mystic animals flies all over the world notifying the members of the medicine company. Mundane creatures—bear, fox, porcupine, and wolf—and smaller species of birds—chickadee, junco, hummingbird—all have the power of transformation and act as humans. Indeed, as Alexander Goldenweiser (1922: 192) pointed out, "among the Iroquois, guardian spirits, whether of animals, birds, or objects, almost always appear in human form. This is in keeping with the highly anthropomorphized character of Iroquois religion, mythology, and cosmology."

Bundle Holders and Cures

Enormous prestige and awesome responsibility accrue to holders of Little Water Society bundles. Besides the principal bundle, during the 1930s on the Allegany Reservation at least three and possibly five smaller packets were held by individuals, of whom three were women.[1] Two women held the old kind. There were several more packets at

---

1. Female bundle holders brought their packets to the renewal ceremony but, because of the strong menstrual taboo, sat in an adjoining room, away from the singers and the combined bundle.

Cattaraugus, the other reservation of the Seneca Nation, and at least two bundles were at Tonawanda, the third Seneca community. In addition, there were bundles at Onondaga (near Syracuse), and the bundle at Six Nations on the Grand River in Canada was attributed to an Allegany source.

Arriving at Coldspring on the Allegheny River below Salamanca, New York, in June 1933, my first experience was not being invited to attend the singing for the medicine. That evening, my host begged off "to go below a mile and a half to help fix the medicine," saying, "Only those who belong may come in." A few evenings later, in a reversal of form, he suddenly asked me—to his wife's consternation—"Would you like to see my *niga:negaʔa:h?*" He sent his young son upstairs to fetch a small suitcase, from which my host took a small bundle of cotton sheeting tied by the corners in two square knots. His wife requested that we go outside. The son ran outside by the rain barrel and joked about it, but he was obviously frightened. My host carefully untied the first wrapping, then a second, to reveal an envelope of Indian tobacco, a small pine spatula, and a pigskin disk, with another revolving within it (once a coin purse), which he turned until a small opening revealed the medicine, a yellowish powder of minute specks, of which indeed there was very little. "When someone is sick," he said, "put a little bit in water that has been dipped with the stream [that is, in the direction of the stream's flow]. If it stands still, he will die; if it sinks to the bottom or turns counterclockwise, he will recover. It is often drunk. It is used for violent injuries and broken bones." This was beginner's luck, for I was never again to see so closely the medicine about which I was to hear so much. For I always listened when bundle holders or beneficiaries talked about it.

Such anecdotes convey better than general statements the way in which the Senecas themselves regard the medicine. They say it is dangerous to ridicule the medicine or make sport of it. "If the medicine is not sung to so many times a year, it will revert upon the best loved of its keepers." This prophecy was later to be fulfilled. The son of a keeper told me: "Once a woman came here from Onondaga to buy some medicine. There was not enough in the main bundle, so I was sent to another place, where they sang over it before giving it away. If the medicine is not properly sung over, it will return. Another time someone put some in a tree some 250 miles away and drove in a plug after it, and next day it was back in the buckskin bag where it was kept. When the medicine is sung over, it replies. When it is put in water, if it turns immediately, the man will recover; if not, it cannot be turned with a paddle."

The taboos on holding the medicine are strict, and the holder should know how to administer it. The requirements are, in fact, so strict that very few persons can comply. Jesse Cornplanter, a learned singer from Newtown then living at Tonawanda, once recounted:

> My father once told me that the rigors of holding the medicine are great. If you are a holder, you cannot take the life of any living thing. Not even a snake. It is the habit of some people when walking along a wooded path to break off a twig in passing. Even this is forbidden to holders, who may not destroy the substance of nature.
>
> It is forbidden to a holder to bear evil thoughts of his fellow beings or to make rash remarks about a person in evil temper.
>
> Some Indians are natural-born singers. They always have some song in mind that they are humming. It is forbidden to hum the tune of a song belonging to the Little Water rituals. Should a ritual tune break into the holder's consciousness, that is a bad sign—some serious injury will befall him or his next of kin. He might cut himself or break a leg. Should this occur, one should invoke the medicine by burning tobacco to break the spell. Even to dream of the song is ominous.
>
> A holder must not drink. Alcohol burns the life strength of the medicine. [Likewise, drunks may not attend meetings or visit a secluded patient.]
>
> A holder may enjoy family life and need not be continent.
>
> The medicine must be kept hidden. No one may touch it or even see it, especially women during menses, who may not attend ceremonies.

My father had to give up the medicine because of the many rigid requirements with which he felt he could not comply. He would not let me attend the meetings, fearing I would learn the songs and inadvertently hum one during my waking moments. I have seen father come down early from the loft where he slept, having dreamt of one of the songs. He would put tobacco in the fire and invoke the charm animals as they requested. Only medicine holders know how.

Cures

The laconic testimony of a famous keeper at Coldspring whom I interviewed sets the clinical boundaries for using the Little Water medicine: "In administering the medicine, the doctor goes to water, dips with the stream, fills a cup three-quarters full, and then places three tiny spots of the sacred powder on the surface. These spots represent the two eyes and mouth of the patient. If the spots revolve counterclockwise, it is a good omen; otherwise one had best throw it out. Three doses are given to the patient—night, morning, and next night, when the body of singers come to help out. The medicine is taken by mouth, and the doctor sprays some of the solution on the patient from his mouth."

In the case of a broken bone, the doctor blew on a white cloth that was wrapped about the fracture. No splints were applied.

Some years later, when I had regularly attended the ceremonies for renewing the medicine, the keeper's daughter, a beneficiary of the medicine and a believer in its power, commented on her father's practice:

When I was a little girl, I wanted to see how father cured people with *niga:negaʔa:h*. I followed father and mother when they went to cure a man who got into a drunken brawl near Red House and was stabbed in the throat through his windpipe. He was left on the Erie Railroad tracks to die where the train might run over him. Aroused by the rumbling of an approaching train, he managed to roll off the track and down the bank into the ditch, where he was found next morning. They brought him home to die.

People had no medical doctor in those days and no hospital. But they sent for my father to administer the Little Water medicine.

When we arrived [the patient] looked like a dead person. He had lost much blood; it oozed from the wound. Father opened the bundle and with a tiny paddle put some of the medicine on the surface of a cup of water. He took some in his mouth and sprayed the wound with medicine water. He gave the patient some to drink, but it came out of the wound through the severed windpipe. So father put some of the medicine inside the wound with the paddle, poked the windpipe and esophagus back into place, and closed the wound. Then he sprayed all over and covered the wound with a white cloth.

It healed in a few days, and in ten days the patient was up and around.

This man was very much alive during the 1930s, when he appeared at Coldspring Longhouse at the Indian New Year to observe the ceremonies. He bore the scar of his wound. Others confirmed his cure.

Members of a bundle holder's family sooner or later get involved. The same daughter continued: "Holders must take great care lest the medicine become restive. My father once came home from curing someone. He was getting old and forgetful, and he had put the packet in the watch pocket of his overalls. I told him to change to clean ones. He discarded the soiled ones in a pile of laundry. The next night he heard the whistle [that is blown in the rite]. He thought it was something outside and disregarded it. He kept hearing it at intervals during the next two days and nights. Then he wondered where had he left the medicine and searched his pockets. He heard the whistle again and discovered the packet in the soiled overalls!"

The shrill whistle was but a portent of other warnings of worse to come. A sibling heard a woman's voice singing during the renewal rite. Several others present also heard it, although no woman was present in the lodge. The old man interpreted this sign as an omen that someone would soon die. His family exhibited considerable anxiety over possessing the bundle and its responsibilities. Gossip in the community held that the keeper had sold some of the medicine while visiting Grand River for the Handsome Lake preachings. And people suspected that I might be interested in acquiring the remainder for a museum.

Within a year after the old man allegedly sold the medicine in bits and pieces, various of his kindred became victims of horrible accidents in automobiles, on the farm, and in industry (Congdon 1967: 147). For the devout these were neither ordinary accidents nor the consequences of working at dangerous occupations. They were ascribed to the operation of the medicine for its neglect and alienation.

Clairvoyance and Witchcraft

In Iroquois society the clairvoyant or fortune-teller performs a powerful role in maintaining the ceremonies of the medicine societies (Shimony 1961a: 261, 1961b). The ethnologist living in a conservative Iroquois community soon becomes aware of their presence and people's dependence on them. During the 1930s at Coldspring, a widow living at Quaker Bridge was the person responsible for what went on to help the sick and the lovelorn. It was said that this old woman and a leading singer of medicine society rites were always cooking up a feast so that she could get a fee and he could eat pig's head. She also held a bundle of the Little Water medicine. The old woman spoke little English, but I found her garrulous in Seneca. Fortunately for me, her niece and understudy was bilingual. For some reason that I could not fathom, they revealed some of the dark secrets of their wicked trade.

On the positive side, the old woman knew her medicine to be effective in cases of accidents, and on occasion she helped the keeper administer it, since he knew little about it. But she cautioned that teasing the medicine would displease it and bring retaliation. She added that a certain matron, a longhouse officer, was unafraid and ridiculed the medicine. Few Senecas, or other Iroquois, in my experience, would take this risk.

The same informant assured me that one would have good luck if one regularly fed the medicine: "Prepare hulled corn soup and sweetened pea-beans, and provide lemon cookies, or white bread, and berry juice. Put a little of each in white teacups without spoons and let stand over night. In the morning throw the despirited food into the river where the water animals can partake of it and where land animals, especially cats and dogs, cannot get at it. The remaining food can be eaten. If the medicine is not fed often, it will harm its keeper, who might get cut with an ax or have some other accident. Or it will consume your blood until you are but skin and bones."

Acts of witchcraft are invariably attributed to other persons. My informants knew just how others used the Little Water medicine for this nefarious purpose. References to specific cases at Coldspring and Tonawanda follow; Annemarie Shimony (1970) described similar cases at Six Nations.

A general lassitude or listlessness is a sure sign that one is being witched. My clairvoyant mentor advised me:

People around here [Allegany] use the medicine to wreak bad luck on another person and to "spoil" things in another household. Specifically, to cause a child to turn over in its mother's womb, one would open the bundle, rest the medicine near the fire, and, while burning tobacco, say: "You know how it fares with that woman yonder. Let her have bad luck, let her child turn over [in her womb]. Cause this to surely happen soon."

Or you can tell the medicine to spoil another person's garden. Her crops will wither.

Indeed, if you yourself do not feel like working or weeding your garden, that is a sign that the medicine is working on you. To counter a spell, burn tobacco and tell the spell to go back where it originated and stay there. "Let it spoil the garden of whoever cast the spell. Let it not interfere with my behavior, but allow me to enjoy good luck." Then your garden will grow and you will feel up to weeding it.

Dreams and Accidents

The Little Water Medicine Society has two classes of members: first, "the adopters" (*tcinonkden?go:wa*), whom I infer are persons who dreamed of the rite or had it prescribed for them, and second, persons who have taken the cure (*-tcinokden?*), often because of accidents.

The importance of dreams in Iroquois life—in revealing the wishes of the soul and compelling fulfillment of specific ceremonies —has been reported from the earliest times (Wallace 1958). To dream of hearing the Little Water songs, to dream of any of the animals that belong to the medicine company (the so-called Society of Mystic Animals [Parker 1909]), or to dream of a pig's head (the feast food) or any of the supporting ritual equipment is a sure sign that the Little Water Society should perform a cure. Or a clairvoyant, interpreting these dreams differently, might prescribe one of the ranked rites of *i:?do:s,* the ceremony that celebrates cures by the Little Water Society.

On two occasions at Allegany I witnessed rites to release the medicine following a cure and confinement. Each case was different. In the summer of 1933, a man was struck in the ear by a foul ball while watching a baseball game at the Coldspring Longhouse ball ground. The blow cut his ear badly, and he suffered a concussion that impaired the sight of his right eye. He was taken to the Salamanca hospital, where the wound was sutured, and his concussion partly cleared. Afterward, his sight bothered him. A month later he solicited the aid of the Little Water Society. One matron said that he should have enlisted the society immediately. Whether to seek traditional aid first or last is always a problem for Longhouse adherents.

Years later, in a parallel case at Six Nations in Canada, a man fell and broke his tibia while scrambling for the "ghost bread" (fried bread) that is tossed outside at intermission during an *?ohgi:weh* (Feast of the Dead) ceremony. The patient told me he had relied first on the "great good medicine," and only after the several days of seclusion did he call in the surgeon of Ohsweken to set the bone. By that time his leg had swollen badly. The surgeon, who had been reared among the Six Nations from boyhood, understood and was sympathetic. When I interviewed him next day, he told me the fracture would have been easier to manipulate earlier. The patient was equally certain that he had followed the right course and ascribed his recovery to the medicine, with an assist by the surgeon.

I interviewed the victim of the foul ball three weeks after the release of the medicine. The doctor of the society had administered the medicine, which he prepared by taking one scoop that held about one grain of the medicine and placing it on the surface of a teacup of water. The patient did not witness the water scrying. The doctor applied some of the solution as a wash: "It felt like a hot towel, although it was cold." The balance was given to the patient to drink. The doctor then bandaged the ear. No singing accompanied the spreading of the Little Water medicine, although sometimes, while the doctor blows the medicine on the patient, singers strengthen the act. It depends on the nature of the injury.

The patient spoke freely of his case:

> The first dose was at night, and then I had to go to bed. I ate nothing before sleeping, although I might have. I was told not to eat vegetables, particularly "our life supporters" [*dyonhehkonh,* corn, beans, and squash], but that my diet should consist of flour dumplings. No salt, sugar, or pork. No milk. The odor of meat should not be permitted close by.
>
> My seclusion lasted three days, although some say four is correct. I remained indoors and did not see my half-sister. This was forbidden. [A woman should not come close to the patient or to the medicine.] During the three days, the doctor visited mornings and evenings. He dressed the wound and fixed a fresh dose of the medicine each evening. I remained in solitary confinement two days, and on the third I went out. It took a week for the wound to heal.

On the third day of this patient's treatment, the society met at the home of the headwoman of the society to release the medicine.

Treatment and cure by the medicine made the patient eligible for membership in the Little Water Society.

Rite to Release the Medicine

In the summer of 1934, while resident in the household of Henry Redeye near Quaker Bridge, I became both participant in and observer of a release ceremony. (Another release had occurred several days before my arrival that summer, after a similar cure in the community.) This ritual is called *sa:wennon?tga:?,* and it is a form of *i:?do:s,* the celebration of the cure. The case involved a member of the Hawk clan in the extended family of my hostess and interpreter, Clara Redeye, Henry's son's wife. The little girl had long suffered from rickets. During a long stay in hospital she had improved, but upon coming home her condition had deteriorated. The old people did not know what was wrong with her. Four days before the release ceremony, someone decided that she should receive the Little Water medicine. Neither Clara nor Sherman Redeye, Henry's son, knew at the time that the little girl had been given the medicine, inasmuch as only the doctor, the woman designated to take care of the patient, and the invoker need be present at the cure.

The occasion for my learning about this was the visit early one morning of the headman of the society, Wadi:je?, to ask Sherman Redeye to sing the release songs and to ask the old man, Henry, to give the tobacco invocation. The visitor whispered to each man in turn.

The release ceremony adheres to a formal structure or pattern of sequence, which I outline here and follow in describing the ceremony.

A. Preliminaries
    1. Headman decides on the ritual for releasing the patient and the medicine
    2. Invites singers
    3. Invites an invoker

B. The ritual of release
    1. Thanksgiving
    2. Tobacco invocation
    3. Smoking tobacco
    4. Singing the ritual
    5. Thanking participants
    6. Feast
        a. Berry juice
        b. Pork
        c. Corn soup

Clara, my hostess and interpreter, continued to fill me in:

After the medicine is administered, the patient must remain in seclusion for four days. Only one person may see her. The patient may eat only mush, made of flour and water. No salt or grease. They make a bread without baking soda or salt. She may drink only water. The designated nurse may be anyone who is living there. Alice Jones [Hawk clan] was taking care of her own daughter.

Both the release ceremony for this little girl and the *i:ʔdo:s* celebration for Jack Dowdy at Alice White's last summer, in which they danced *sawonnonʔtga:ʔ,* serve the same purpose, to let the medicine go. The procedure to be used tonight is merely simpler and does not require dance leaders or attendance by the society. Each rite has its own songs.

Clara thought the songs were taken from the repertoire of songs sung at the triennial meetings of the society to renew the medicine.

Sherman agreed that he would sing one group of three to four selected songs. Just which variety of *i:ʔdo:s* songs is performed is up to the headman, who selects the ritual to release the medicine. The singer evidently selects the songs. A similar selection from the "water spreading songs" is sung when the medicine is first administered.

Terminology: *i:ʔdo:s,* the generic name of the celebration cere-

mony; *hadi:ʔdo:s,* "they are performing that ceremony," or the name
of the society; *oenoiʔah,* "song of release"; *sawonnonʔtga:ʔ,* a branch of
i:ʔdo:s, a word the Senecas today elide to *sawenonʔgaʔ.*

After the preliminaries have been conducted and the participants
invited, the actual ceremony proceeds as follows:

1. Thanksgiving, the general greeting and thanksgiving from
earth to sky (*ganon:yonk*) (Chafe 1961). When we were all gathered
at the house of confinement, Henry Redeye greeted us with a familiar speech that precedes all gatherings in Iroquois society.

2. Tobacco invocation. Matters grew serious with the tobacco
invocation. Henry specified why we were met and what the ceremony of release should accomplish. He dictated the Seneca text to
me afterward, Sherman and Clara interpreted, and the English translation follows.

> So now the smoke arises from the Indian tobacco which our
> Creator intended that the people should use so that they might
> be heard through it, as he himself, Our Creator, intended.
>
> So now, there is a certain matter to which you shall listen,
> namely, the thing here [the medicine] that helps us continually.
> Just three nights ago they pleaded with you to help someone.
> You all were fortunate that this thing helped her. So therefore
> you are released, and now rightly he who took care of you now
> is responsible [for the care of the medicine],[2] and rightly you
> shall look to him for instruction, for surely it shall always pos-
> sess your body of this [person] we call "flying about" [*gadje:san,*
> Hawk clan].[3]
>
> So now then he has fulfilled what you [the medicine]
> required, namely, the keeper has fulfilled the rite of spreading

---

2. According to Clara Redeye, Henry Redeye has freed the medicine by burning
tobacco; now it is up to the man who is guardian of the medicine (the *hodane:t,* Hiram
Watt) to take charge of it for the society.

3. When one drinks the medicine, it will always remain in one's system—it never
gets out; the medicine will always possess her body. Here the medicine is really speaking, not the speaker himself.

tobacco.[4] This very night she [the patient] has met the reqire-
ments;[5] she has provided berry juice with which the medicine
society members shall greet each other.[6]

She has also provided a piece of meat, literally carrion, for
us to pick at. It is a piece of meat cut from the body of a bear,
which was formerly traveling back and forth on the ground.
And this cut of meat will presently go around counterclockwise, as they pick at it like crows.[7]

So now she has prepared and set down a kettle of hulled
corn soup. She has fulfilled everything with which she will
thank all of you.

So now then they pray that the medicine shall in that way
continue to help her in the future.

The [medicine] will merely perform the rite of release.[8]

So the medicine company will sing only the brief songs of
release, for only so much is required for the medicine to feel
favorably disposed. This bit of tobacco partakes [savors] the rite
of release.

Therefore everything pertaining to the *i:ʔdo:s* ceremony
[of which the release ceremony is a part] partakes of the
tobacco: all of the songs belonging to it receive tobacco, and
also the great round dance. Everything relating to *i:ʔdo:s* par-

---

4. The interpreter thought the speaker made a mistake here, for the reference to
spreading tobacco refers to the regular meetings of the Little Water Society, when the
tobacco is set down on the floor for the medicine and they sing to strengthen the medicine.

5. The patient who drank the medicine has met the requirements for emerging
from seclusion: setting down tobacco for the medicine and providing berry juice for
the smokers.

6. When the waiters pass the pails of juice, a member says either, "I greet and
thank all of you medicine society members" (*o:tgwano:nyon:ʔ swatcinonhgenʔshonʔ*)—
both performers and spirit-forces—or "I greet and thank our helper, that which helps
us continually" (*otkennon:nyon:ʔ ongwayaʔdagehasheʔ*).

7. Bear meat was the original feast food, as Henry, who favored the old language,
specified, although Clara, my interpreter, thought he surely meant pig's head, the contemporary feast food at medicine society feasts. "The old people used to go at it with
gusto, but now they only pick at it."

8. The use of the word "merely" (*dishon*) indicates that they will merely sing the
songs of release.

takes of the tobacco, including all of the songs attending the great round dance [*ganonyahgwen?go:wa:*], which is the name of the dance when they all go around.

Therefore only so much is required that the tutelaries shall feel favorably disposed toward us. So we plead that you do not let misfortune happen.

So now then this the medicine is returned to the person named "Lodged in a crotch" [Hawetheonk, Hiram Watt, the keeper], who shall take care of it properly, for she [the patient] has also made a bed for it [spread a white cloth]. It is done. So that is all.

3. Smoking of tobacco. Here the participants pause to smoke and then wash away the tobacco taste with berry juice. This bit is called *ondiyen?gowai,* "to wash away tobacco." The headman or conductor passes the berry juice to each participant without speaking. In this role, Hiram Watt remarked, "Whiteman over there, maybe he too will take some berry juice." A person taking the ladle should say, "?Otgwanonnyon swatcinon?gea?shon? [I give thanks to you medicine society performers]" or "?Okenon?nyon? ?ongwaya?dagehashe:? [I return thanks to her (the medicine) that is continually helping us]."

4. Singing the ritual. This part of the release ceremony is called *?ennondeno:den ?enwon?sa:wen?,* "they will commence to sing" (literally, "they the songs will commence").

During songs 1 and 2, the performers were seated as diagrammed in figure 1, about as they were seated during the previous episodes of smoking and passing berry juice. The patient, meanwhile, sat in an adjoining room among her female relatives, including her mother and the wives of the performers. The participants and their roles were as follows (numbers correspond to those in fig. 1).

1. Hiram Watt (Deer clan), headman of the medicine society
2. Sherman Redeye (Snipe clan), first singer
3. Myron Turkey (Turtle clan)
4. Henry Redeye (Bear clan), speaker and invoker

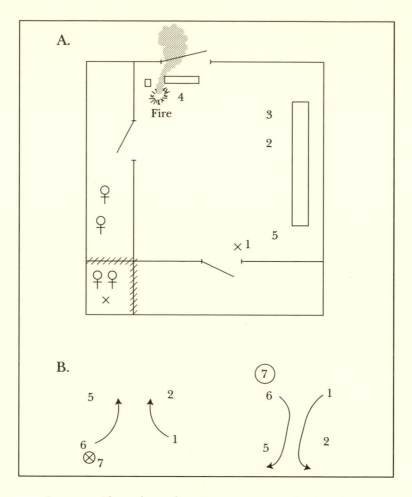

FIGURE 1. Floor plan and seating arrangement for the release
ceremony at Allegany, 1934.

5. Albert Jones (Snipe clan), father of patient, second singer
6. Alice Jones (Hawk clan), mother of patient, nurse
7. Child patient (Hawk clan)

At the third song, they all stood, as shown at the bottom of figure 1:
the lead singer (2) with the second singer (5) opposite; the headman

(1), who had administered the medicine, on the side of the first singer (2); and the nurse (6), carrying the child patient (7), on the side of the second singer (5).

The participants remained seated while singing songs 1 and 2. At the third song they stood and remained standing through songs 3 to 8. The latter section corresponds to the marching songs in *i:ʔdo:s*. As the songs progressed, the headman moved toward the first singer, and the nurse and patient moved beside the second singer, the two sides facing each other.

They stood thus during the first half of the song; then the two singers, shaking their rattles double-time, changed places with the headman and the nurse carrying the child, passing them on the outside to stand in each other's respective places for the balance of the song. Then they repeated the song and routine, returning to their original stations.

Sherman Redeye, having sung the ritual, assured me that the first two songs have no meaningful words, only nonsense vocables. The third song text, however— *ganonhshenʔ hade:he:ʔt*, "in the middle of the house, they both stand," or, as we would say, "The two stand in the middle of the house"—refers to the lead singer and the patient. Songs 4 to 8 again have no meaningful words.

This ceremony involves no special moiety alignment of the clans.

5. Thanking the participants. The father of the patient stood and thanked everyone who took part, without identifying anyone by name. This is the custom. First he thanked the doctor for bringing the medicine and helping the little girl. He thanked him for all that he had done as headman of the society and conductor of its rite of releasing the medicine. Second, he thanked the invoker for "putting tobacco" and pleading to the tutelaries to release the little girl from the medicine and freeing them. Third, he thanked the first singer. And last, he thanked everyone who had come to help with the singing or merely to look on.

6. The feast. The terminal feast that ends all Seneca ceremonies is called, fittingly, "to pass some food around" (*oʔwadjakon*). The menu on this occasion consisted of three items: berry juice, pork, and

hulled corn soup. The headman passed each of these in turn. In serving the hulled corn soup, the father of the patient filled the headman's pail first, before filling the other pails. This duty falls to the patient or to someone acting on his or her behalf. One does not say thanks on receiving his portion of the soup. Learning such bits of etiquette is crucial to getting on in Seneca society.

Historical Precedents

A background of such contemporary cases enables one to evaluate accounts of cures in historical sources. Father Joseph-François Lafitau's early-eighteenth-century account of Mohawk medical practices at Kahnawake (Caughnawaga), outside Montreal, declared the healing of gunshot wounds to be "the masterpiece of their operations and so remarkable as to be almost unbelievable. They concocted a treacle water composed several classes of graduated ingredients: vulnerary herbs, trees, and the bodies and hearts of animals, all in powder form." He also mentioned dietary restrictions and the doctor's taking some of the solution in his mouth before sucking the wound or spraying it. Lafitau attached great importance to the practice of covering the wound so that it avoided contact with everything save a possible binding of boiled herbs. He remarked that the Indians thought this prevented infection. He further noted that when the wounds were dressed and this operation repeated, the wounds always appeared clean, fresh, and free of clots (Lafitau 1977 [1724], 2: 204–5.)

Indeed, the medicine comes down from an earlier time when it comprised the medicine bundle carried by Iroquois war party leaders. At least, this is the tradition: historical documentation is lacking, but folklore is fairly consistent. Old Senecas of a previous generation told Arthur C. Parker (personal communication, June 1933) that Senecas fighting with the British mourned losing their bundle at the Battle of Oriskany in 1777.

◆ 2 ◆

The Origin Legend

The legend of Good Hunter, or "Bloody Hand," which relates the founding of the Little Water Society, exists in many versions, several dating from the nineteenth century. It comes from Seneca, Onondaga, Tuscarora, and Wyandot sources, preceded by a Huron reference of 1636; the published literature suggests that northern Iroquoian people shared the tale and the medicine. With a common plot and characters, the origin myths relate how a council of birds and animals restored life to Good Hunter, who had been scalped and left to die in the woods. They concocted a powder composed of meat cut from the thighs (or hearts) of living animals, who were released, healed themselves, and survived. Later in the chapter I will come back to some of these earlier versions (see Barbeau 1915: 333; Beauchamp 1901: 153; Clarke 1870: 24; Doty 1876: 52; Johnson 1881; Parker 1908; Thwaites 1896–1901, 10: 177). First, I want to present two fuller versions that I collected myself.

My two principal mentors among the Senecas at Coldspring on the origins and rituals of the Little Water Society—John Jimerson and Chauncey Johnny John—derived their learning from Cattaraugus, where traditionalists settled after Buffalo Creek Reservation was abandoned. The version of Jesse Cornplanter, then resident at Tonawanda, belongs to the same genre (Cornplanter 1938: 33). Although few individual Senecas in my experience knew the legend of Good Hunter, I did collect two somewhat different versions.

John Jimerson's Version

Late in the summer of 1934, John Jimerson (Hawk clan) of High Bank instructed me on the origin of the Little Water medicine and then, in September, introduced me to the renewal ceremony at Newtown on Cattaraugus (fig. 2). This was one profound learning

FIGURE 2. John Jimerson (Hawk clan), left, instructs me
on the origins of the Little Water medicine.

experience, worth repeating. Jimerson's English required little editing (WNF Seneca field notes 1934, xv: 1ff.).

> The Senecas were great warriors. They were in the habit of
> going afar scalping, usually toward the Cherokee country.
> Senecas going south met Cherokees coming north, and they
> fought. During the fighting one Seneca warrior got chased. His
> enemies were closing behind him and there was barely room
> for him to pass under a leaning tree. When he straightened on
> the far side, a pursuer could just reach over the leaning tree
> trunk and scalp him.
>
> The escaping Seneca did not notice that he had been
> scalped and kept running. No longer was anyone chasing him,
> but he kept on running in the direction of his home in the
> Seneca country.
>
> When the Seneca warrior reached his native village, he
> was perplexed that people did not look at him. His sweetheart,
> on the way for water, passed him by without speaking. She did
> not see him. No one, not even his closest friends, noticed him
> or even spoke. They seemed not to hear. It surprised him that
> when he spoke people did not hear. Then he felt lonesome, for
> no one noticed that he had returned to the village.
>
> Then he went back to the place where they had been
> fighting in the woods along the trail to the Cherokee country.
> When the warrior arrived at the place where he had been
> scalped, he saw a man lying there. People were gathering and
> sitting in a circle around the body. One man was addressing
> them:[1]
>
> "Now we, our people, have to repay this man. We must
> help to restore him to earth once more because he alone is
> very mindful [thoughtful] of us. Indeed, he loves us. He always
> makes us a present of the whole carcass of a deer whenever he
> goes hunting. He takes the whole body of a deer, rips its belly,
> exposing the entrails, while taking nothing for himself, but
> says, 'Listen, all of you meat eaters. This is for you.' Then he

---

1. In Seneca mythology, animal tutelaries appear in human form.

always leaves the deer carcass and goes on his way. Now we must repay him."

Now the speaker said: "Now anyone may appoint himself [volunteer] to retrieve the scalp."

Now one of the Wolf tribe came forward, saying, "I will go and fetch it." So now they made a council to ascertain who could do it properly so as to determine whether the Wolf was capable of the mission.

Now one person stood and said, "The Wolf cannot accomplish the task, for he lacks sufficient power. The scalp is in a dangerous place," the giant crow said, for he had been flying back and forth across the earth about his business. "The scalp hangs near the smoke hole of the house in the Cherokee village, where the victor stretched it on a hoop and hung it to dry. The Wolf is not fitted to fetch it."

Now another man stood and spoke, saying, "I will go and get it." So they met again in council to investigate whether he was powerful enough to accomplish it. So the Bear volunteered, but he, like the Wolf, lacked the secret power [magic power].

Now another one volunteered: " I will go and fetch it." This time it was *gahga?go:wa:,* the Raven. And they held another council to investigate whether he, too, had power sufficient to the task. And they decided that he, too, was not the proper candidate, for the same reason—he lacked sufficient power.

Now another said, "I will go." This was the common field crow, *ga?ga:?.* After long deliberation, the council granted it; they decided, "Yes, you have the power and are smart [tough] enough. You both have strength and are wily."

Well, the crow went, because this business required haste. The task had to be done quickly, if they were to save this warrior.

So now there were some who remained in council. So now their leader, who was Panther, said: "Now we must go to work and make medicines for him while Crow is gone for the scalp."

"Everyone must bare his breast and cut it open."

The entire council did as they were bid—cutting the skin

and taking out a bit of the breast meat [pectoral muscle]. All who were there did it. They were all kinds of animals, but appearing in human form. They all followed the orders of their leader, cutting out a bit of the meat and setting it aside to dry. All of the blood that issued from their wounds was saved and dried.

When all of the meat and blood had dried—and it dries quickly—they made it into a powder. They had everything ready by the time the crow returned with the scalp.

The crow arrived and made his report, telling what had happened on his journey: "The Cherokee warriors were watching; everything they see, they kill, saying, 'That is the Senecas approaching.' Now I gathered up quite a group [flock] of my people, and I directed them to fly about above the village, over the house where the scalp was drying, but high up, out of range of their arrows. I watched up there from amongst them until finally I got a chance.

"I folded my wings and dropped down through the smoke hole. I snatched the scalp and climbed up again. No one saw me, until I reached where the rest of my people were still flying, lazily circling. Then we flew away without anyone's missing the scalp. So here it is."

And the crow laid the scalp before the council of game animals. Their chief said, "Thanks for doing it. You did well. Now let us go to work and raise up this man."[2]

Meanwhile, the Seneca warrior, having returned to the place where he had passed under the leaning tree, was sitting there amongst the council, but they did not notice him because it was his spirit [*otwaishe?*]; his body lay extended on the ground. The warrior did not perceive or understand, nor did he realize, that it was his own body lying there on the ground.

Now they made the Little Water. The warrior did not notice where they obtained the bucket for the water. They rubbed the scalp with the "small water" to soften it. And they rubbed the place where it had been removed from the patient's head. Panther, as leader, discussed the cure with Raven and

---

2. Edwin M. Loeb treated the theme of death and resurrection in his study "Tribal Initiations and Secret Societies" (1929).

with several huge birds from the cloudy regions who are eaters of meat. Now they sat in a circle where the patient lay extended.

Having finished making the medicine and rubbing the scalp and the wound, Raven, as speaker, arose and said, "Now we are going to sing. Be careful and do not step."[3] (The fallen warrior did not notice where they got their rattles [but they materialized like the buckets a few moments before].)

Now they commenced singing the "water spreader" songs (*go?negonhje:ta?*), which is the name for the first group of songs for administering the medicine, called "spreading water." From a vessel of the "Little Water," they let it trickle drop by drop into the dead man's mouth until they had given him all of it. Meanwhile they kept singing. Then they stopped.

[Intermission]

So now, having finished the first group of water-spreading songs, they rested and smoked. Everyone carried a pouch of tobacco containing a pipe.

Presently the headman said, "Now we will give another dose."

So the Raven went ahead and made another "small water." Meanwhile, the invisible man, sitting amongst them, watched closely. He saw Raven take a tiny paddle (*gagawisha?*) and dip a bit of the powder three times, placing it [on the surface of water] first to the north, second to the south, and third to the west.[4]

They were now singing a second group of water-spread- ing songs [which John knew]. During the fifth song, with the

---

3. "This is as I do when I open the meeting: I am *gahga?go:wa:* [Raven], although I do not know the first group of songs." The caution not to "step," or beat time with one's foot, as Iroquois singers habitually do, reminds the singers of their awesome responsibility.

4. The placement of the powder on the surface of the water can be diagrammed as shown here, with each asterisk representing a bit of powder:

```
              * N 1
    3 W *
              * S 2
```

The figure represents a man looking toward the west. In death they lay the body out with the head toward the west, and the implication is that the medicine is so powerful it can raise a dying person.

paddle one stirs the medicine slowly in a counterclockwise direction. Just then the warrior spirit noticed that the water now revolved rapidly, as if it were animated. The text of the seventh song says, "They give him a drink," and so now they gave him a dose. The observer could see them raise the patient's chin so as to drop the medicine slowly down his throat, while others dressed the scalp wound. They sang a few more songs.

[Second intermission]

Once more the animals rested and smoked. As in recent sessions, they talked and enjoyed themselves, while others went off in the bush. The observer thought they were people and listened to their every word. One, who appeared to be an older fellow, was saying, "This fellow whom we are helping is the one who always helps us by giving us some fresh meat recently killed. Now this man when he goes hunting in the fall season, when he kills his first deer, rips it up and says: "Here it is. Hear me, you meat eaters. This is for you. Here is my first kill which I offer to the meat eaters." Then he went on with his hunting. He always had good luck, for having given his first kill to the meat eaters. We are going to bring him back to life so that he may go about once more on the earth."

The reason this man spoke was to explain to the listening spirit, who would presently return to his body, the purpose of the medicine.

Now the headman announced: "We are going to give him an extra dose."

So now then Raven went to work preparing another small water. When everything was ready, he went to where the man lay and let a few drops of the medicine fall into the patient's mouth. The remainder he used to bathe the scalp. The spirit of the warrior, who all this while sat by unseen, watching the cure, failed to notice how it happened that it was he himself lying there being cured. Now he is back in his body once more, for they have succeeded in bringing his spirit [soul] back to that place.[5]

---

5. This sentence expresses the belief that the soul can be restored to the body by the power of song.

Now the speaker stood and said, "So now then all of you members of the medicine society, listen. Now we are going to sing, to strengthen what we have accomplished."

Now the warrior was thinking, "It is about midnight now that he [the headman] has finished." He had noticed that they had procured a bucket, but he did not perceive where it came from. Now they drink a bucket of berry juice, which they also bring forth, thanking our Creator and the Appointed Ones for everything that has been ordained and created on this earth.[6]

Now the speaker told everyone to sing. "Everyone must sing as best he can. Let no one hear the pads when their feet hit." [The mystic animals do not beat their feet, and neither are human singers supposed to bump their feet during ritual singing.]

After he had finished speaking, the servants, who are Eagles [*jo:nyondah*] and next in rank to headman Raven, who ranks beneath Panther, the high chief, pick up the buckets of berry juice and pass them around to the singers. The waiters also do the cooking, fix the berry juice, serve, and tend the doors. The other servant is Wolf [*tha:yo:nih*], who acts as runner to summon the members to meetings, which Raven conducts.

At this point, John projected his knowledge of contemporary ritual practice into the era of mythology:

All the members of the society drink in turn, commencing with the singers, who say, "I return thanks to all that grows," or "I thank you, Thunders," or "I thank the luminaries, including the stars," or "I thank the Four Persons" [the Appointed Ones], or "We thank you, our Creator," or "I thank that which helps us" [the medicine]. This last was said on behalf of the man [the Good Hunter].

---

6. Here the narrator uses the present tense because he is projecting his ritual knowledge into the myth.

When they had all partaken of the berry juice, they commenced singing the first group, *djojen?dahgon*.

The Good Hunter was amazed to hear such a loud and high-pitched song, thinking to himself, "They will hear that far off."

(The animals did not have a whistle, which imitates the voice of the birds who then were singing. Some birds above us sing that way. We are only now able to imitate the voice of the cloud dwellers like Dew Eagle.)

Having finished the first group of songs, they stopped to rest. Good Hunter noticed that there was no light during the singing, but when they rested, the light was more brilliant than daylight. He thought that he had never heard such great speakers as those who talked during the intermission. They passed the berry juice, and then the speaker announced that they would sing the second group of songs.

They sing the second group, *dekni:wadonta?*.

Having again finished singing, they rested. The headman said, "Now we will rest a short while and smoke." Good Hunter was amazed: it seems that they made a cloud when they smoked. He had never seen such great smokers. "These people esteem smoking above all else." Now the singers got up again [and hit the bush] while the servants passed the bucket of juice. They returned thanks to each other and to this man for whom they were singing.

The headman announced: "Now we resume singing, this time a third group."

They sing the third group of songs, *?o:denoga:de?*. The third group is longest and has the most songs.

Having now finished singing the third group, the speaker said, "Now we will rest again, have another smoke, and then have another drink."

It was already late autumn, when war parties went out, and the Good Hunter could not understand where they got the berries, and he had not yet fathomed where they got the bucket.

Now the headman said, "We are going to sing once more.

This will be the last time."

They sing the fourth group of songs, *heyenongai:dasta?*. These are the ending [closing] songs.

During the singing, Good Hunter began to feel alive. He commenced moving his arms, then his legs, and his head. He felt normal. When they finish that group, the lead singer says, "?edwaiyose?"—it is ended [we are finished].

Now the speaker rises and says: "Indeed, now it is finished—every word that we had to fulfill. Now we are through with him. Now he shall travel to and fro on the earth."

Now the headman addressed the patient: "I am going to tell you all about this secret powder that we are going to let you take with you so that your people may be helped. You already understand everything that we have done [to restore you to life]. You must teach your people, instructing them to honor the medicine, and not fool with it. You must sustain it as long as your people survive. If at any time your supply of the medicine is short, you know what kind of ingredients to seek. Your own people can make it themselves. You understand that all of it should be taken from the chest: a piece of meat, a little blood—dry and powder it.

"Now then another thing. You must strengthen the medicine by singing for it every four months. Singing keeps the medicine fresh. And straighten up the bundles. This renews the strength of every portion. This substance is for the protection of your people from invisible ways, for they will never know if some unforeseen event is coming toward them. Perhaps, an accident [*adiwajeonshe?*]."

Now the Good Hunter noticed that it was brightening: dawn was approaching. The morning star was already above the horizon.

Then the speaker added, "We are going to stand revealed and let you see us. And then when we all disperse, you must go home to your household. And when you are nearing home, cry as if you were approaching the village: 'Ko:weh ko:weh ko:weh!'" [This was the death cry of a returning war party.]

"When you have reached the village and everyone has

shaken your hand, then you must relate to them all of your experiences, all that you have seen, and all that we have told you. The power of the powder that you will take will serve as a great protection when you go out to fight.

"Now it is entirely finished.

"Now when you go hunting, you must continue the way you have been doing. We are ever grateful for the fresh meat that you sacrifice. You will continue to be a successful hunter, always having good luck.

"Now one other thing. When you wish to use the medicine, burn tobacco, as you do in sacrificing the deer, and tell the medicine what you expect of it." (The council of animals had not burned tobacco. Their performance was really the medicine itself. They merely smoked.)

Now the Good Hunter stood, and he felt more alive standing, more so than ever before. Then every one of the council of animals also stood and, turning, started to go. When they turned, that was the last time they appeared as humans. They transformed into animals and stood revealed as all of the dangerous meat-eating animals.[7]

The Good Hunter watched the meat eaters depart. Then he went home to tell his people. The headman of the village gathered the people into the council house to hear the hunter relate his adventure. He told them that he had already been there once, but no one recognized him. When he spoke, no one heard him. Disgusted and lonely, he went back to the place of the leaning tree on the path to the Cherokee country, where he noticed for the first time the fallen man. He did not recognize that it was himself.

Then he related his cure by the animals.

"So that is all of it."

But there was more to it. Tradition took over where folklore ended.

---

7. Transformation occurs in Seneca myths whenever the anthropomorphic spirits turn to go. Then they assume their animal forms.

The War Bundle in History

The Little Water Society and its celebration rite, *i:ʔdo:s,* formerly functioned in the Iroquois war complex. John Jimerson said: "Centuries ago, *i:ʔdo:s* and the Little Water bundle were used for war purposes. When they went out scalping, they made up a war party, and their leader carried a bundle of the Little Water medicine together with a gourd rattle. When the party turned in for the night, the leader hung the bundle, together with the rattle, in a tree. Next morning the leader would look at the bundle. Having examined it, he could say, 'All right, we can go on.' Sometimes a rattle dropped to the ground and broke. Then the chief would say, 'Now we have had bad luck, we must return.' They could not continue, for surely misfortune would befall them."

This account is reminiscent of the Winnebago practice reported for the Great Lakes area (Radin 1916). John did not mention planting a crotched pole to elevate the bundle and rattles in the manner of contemporary Eagle Dance Society practice (Fenton 1953: Plate 21).

Evidently, both the Little Water Society and the Eagle Dance Society were formerly war societies. Later on, when the wars ceased, some people who liked the songs and the way the warriors danced urged them to perform. Later they became ill. "It went into their blood."

"Then we had good clairvoyants," whom people consulted. "They brought presents of Indian tobacco, and sometimes silver ornaments, usually brooches. The clairvoyant might say, 'You go home and return for the word in the water' [divination by water scrying]. Then the clairvoyant slept and had a vision that instructed him."

The clairvoyant prescribed: "You must have corn soup; you must procure a bear's head; you must prepare berry juice, provide chunks of meat for the singers, and above all Indian tobacco. When you have supplied all of that, call upon the company of medicine holders, the *honontcinohgenʔ,* afford a place for them to meet, and let them sing for you."

"After the dance, the woman patient who sponsored the first meeting got up without resort to other medicines."

And this is the beginning of *i:ʔdo:s,* which belongs together with the "small water" [*niga:negaʔa:h*].

Chauncey Johnny John's Version

During the 1930s and until his death in the 1950s, Chauncey Johnny John reigned as lead singer for the Little Water Society. I had known Chauncey since the collecting activities of my father during the 1920s, and early in my fieldwork he undertook to teach me the elements of Iroquois ethnobotany and the mysteries of the medicine societies. His version of the origin of the Little Water medicine compares interestingly with John Jimerson's. It features the same plot, but in a different style with new elements.

I have forgotten the name of the man who first used that medicine. It is too long ago. I am an old man now [1938]. My father [Abraham Johnny John of Cattaraugus] told me the legend, and so I tell my grandson and you because I know that you will tell no one else around here.[8]

There used to be a little Indian village, and so they held a council. The headman summoned the warriors to meet, and when they gathered, he said, "We must go to the next village. It is quite distant. We are going up there and scalp them." That people were called *ʔoya:daʔ* (Cherokee) [*ʔoyataʔke:aʔ,* "cave people" (Chafe 1963: 35)].

Then they set out.

It seems that one man who always went on the warpath, named Donishohgwageh:wenʔ, joined the raid [*wainonhgiʔwa:*]. When they reached the Cherokee town, they had a battle.

---

8. How to resolve the conflict between informant confidence and the ethnologist's obligation to science poses a question of ethics. I believe that Chauncey's heirs today need not be deprived of his wisdom.

Now it seems that for the first time this man, who had been to war many times and returned, was killed and scalped.

He lay there where he had fallen for two or three days. It was one of the animals who called all of the animals to assemble where he lay. This animal said, "I think we had best help this man because during a great many days he has helped us. Whenever he used to hunt and killed game, he habitually cut it open and flayed it and called all of the predators to come and get some meat. Whereupon he went away and looked for another game animal for himself. Therefore I think we should help him now."

So they did. "Let us help him," they all said.

[Eagle Baiting]

So now then, addressing the two animals next to him, the speaker [headman] said: "Go to the top of yonder hill." They [three] went up there together. The headman called upon Dew Eagle [ʔoshadaʔgeːaʔ] [ʔoshataʔkeːaʔ (Chafe 1953: 58)] to come down and have some meat. Turning to his two accomplices, the headman instructed one: "You hide there." And to the other: "You hide on the opposite side." Accordingly, the two hid close to where the meat lay.

Dew Eagle was a long time descending to the meat. At last he stooped and looked about for anyone lurking nearby. He saw no one. Then he approached the meat. When alongside, he looked about a second time, and when he saw no one, he snatched at the meat, cutting off a piece. Then he looked about once more. Presently he took a second piece, repeating the behavior, and again a third piece. When he bent his head down, one of the hidden men [animals] rushed out and grabbed him, and the second one jumped out, and together the two pinioned the bird. One of them addressed the bird: "Be quiet! I am going to tell you what we are about to do." So Dew Eagle listened. "We are going to help this man lying here who used to help us."

Dew Eagle replied, "All right, we can do that."

And so they four descended to where the man lay. The headman of the animals, addressing Dew Eagle, said: "You got here all right," and Dew Eagle answered, "Yes. I sent two men to fetch you to come down here because I want to help this man who has been killed and scalped. The reason I want to help him is the custom he used to observe when hunting. Whenever he killed game, he opened it and called us to come and eat, which we did. Now we must help this man." Dew Eagle agreed.

[The Cure]

So now the headman, the one who does all the talking, pointed to the scalped man. "Can you fix that?" He summoned Wolf and directed him: "You clean this wound." And Wolf licked the wound clean. "Now," he said, "I want two fellows—two crows [*deknigahga:*] to come down." He instructed them: "You two must go and fetch his scalp, which is hanging in the middle of the [Cherokee] village from the tip of a great long pole. Bring it back here. When you return carrying scalps, cry out [the scalp cry: *ko:weh ko:weh!*]." So they went.

At last they heard the two crows hollering. When the council of animals discerned them coming, they saw that they were carrying the old man's scalp. When they arrived, Wolf cleaned it and once more licked the scalp wound clean there where the hunter lay.

Then the headman of the council of animals called upon the Bear—"You, come over here"—which he did. "You put this scalp back where it was torn off."You see, the Bear can use his hands like a human. That is why the headman asked him to do it.

Next the speaker turned to Dew Eagle. "You come over here and give the man some medicine." Dew Eagle went there and spit on the wound where the scalp came off. Saliva rolled down over the hunter's skull, healing the wound quickly and completely.[9] And all the while the headman, the animal that does all the talking, was singing the Little Water songs.[10]

[The Healing Songs]

---

9. In other versions the bird regurgitates on the scalp and the head wound. Perhaps Chauncey meant this but said "spit."

10. These are the "water-spreading songs" of the healing ritual. This version fails to mention gourd rattles, which singers now employ.

Presently the headman observed, "He is recuperating, keep on singing." So they kept singing.

Not long after, the dead man heard something while lying there. But yet he could not distinguish what was going on. He lay still. Presently he heard someone talking about him, saying, "He is going to get well soon. He will recover." Still later, the hunter sat up, and now for the first time he saw those animals ranged around him. It was then that he noticed who had been conducting this affair. We call him *hen:es*—panther—who had been in charge [*hasdei:sdon?*]. Panther asked him, "Are you all right now?" The hunter responded, "I guess that I will be all right after a while."

And so this headman, the boss of the animals, said: "We will fix you so that you will be all right soon." At that he sent two assistants for water. They went and fetched the water. They carried it in their mouths, for they had no buckets. They gave him some of it to drink. After he drank, he commenced to feel better.

The hunter now sat up on the log of a fallen tree. He noticed his weapons— his bow and arrows, tomahawk, and scalping knife—lying on the ground where he fell. He picked them up.

The headman said, "You may go now." So he departed.[11]

[Hunting Customs]

Presently the hunter stopped near a creek and put up camp, where he stayed overnight. Next morning he went out a little way to hunt. He took game, a deer. Accordingly he proceeded as was his custom. He flayed it and hollered: "Come all who crave meat." And then he set out to take another deer for himself. Soon he felled another small young one. It seems that he tried to carry it whole but was unable to lift it. So he looked about with the intent of getting basswood bark. He found a basswood pole [sapling] and peeled away the bark for a leash. He made a hole in the deer's nostrils [septum], inserted one end of the bark, and tied it. And so he dragged the fawn back to camp,

---

11. This version does not witness the transformation of the actors to animals.

where he skinned it. He broiled some of the meat for his evening meal. And after he was done eating he went to bed on hemlock boughs and covered himself with the pelt.

As he lay there he heard something in the bush. A voice outside inquired, "Are you asleep?" The hunter replied, "Nearly."

The voice outside continued: "Then I think that you had better wait because I want to talk with you." Coming in and sitting opposite across the fire, the person went on: "They sent me here to instruct you concerning the medicine that we used when you were lying there in the forest." Then the stranger asked, "Have you tobacco?" The hunter replied, "I have a little."[12]

The visitor commented, "Perhaps that will be sufficient."

[Summoning the Medicine Company]

The hunter gave the tobacco to the visitor. So now then this person, who was an animal appearing in human form and behavior, who indeed represented the medicine company, sprinkled tobacco on the fire to summon all of the animals on earth, and all of the birds clear up to the Cloud-dweller, or Dew Eagle. "We are going to instruct this man about the medicine." He called upon Giant Crow, or Raven, to come down.[13] And when Raven landed, the speaker charged him, "Go down west and tell all of the animals on earth to come here. When you have finished there, go east and do likewise."[14] So they alerted all of the animals to listen as the speaker cast tobacco and informed them what would happen. "Every one of you bring your medicine." So they all gathered up their medicine and brought it there.

When they were assembled, the speaker instructed the hunter, "When you reach home, you are going to prepare a

12. This follows the pattern for Seneca origin legends. Following an adventure, the tutelary appears to the hunter in a dream to impart further instructions.

13. Giant Raven is messenger for the medicine company and the title of the person who summons members to meetings.

14. This summons is still employed whenever the medicine society meets. The messenger who performs the role of *gahga?go:wa:* notifies the members by placing a kernel of corn in each member's hand.

medicine that is composed of ingredients derived from the hearts of all the animals. We prepare it now so that you can reproduce it when you get home.

"I shall return tomorrow night."

[Here the narrator repeats, for effect, the hunting incident of the previous day, including the events and conversations that lead us to the revelation.]

So now it happened again, at dusk when the hunter was in camp. When he was nearly asleep, a voice from outside inquired: "Are you awake?" "Yes," the hunter replied. The voice continued: "I am here this time to teach you the songs." He commenced singing and went through what we call "one period" [*dyogohsa:t*], with the company repeating each song after him. When he had gone through one period, the singer rested and smoked. So they did. They both smoked.

Presently they commenced again. When they had completed the second period [*dekniwadonta:ʔ*], they rested again and smoked.

Once more, the speaker announced, "We are to start another period. This time we are going to finish. It will be the final period." So they completed it. When they had finished singing, the instructor arose and asked the hunter whether he knew any of the songs. The hunter replied, "Yes, I know some of them."

Then the instructor thanked all of the animals, every one of them who had participated. He threw tobacco again, telling them that they had been thanked.

The first night the headman was alone, but all of the animals returned with him the second night, and they all took part in the singing. A great buck deer, the oldest buck in the woods, led the singing. (The first leader had been Panther.)

The headman said, "We had best continue to help the people as long as the waters flow and the sun shines. This man is going to make a medicine for his people like the medicine that we made for him. In order that his people shall keep up the medicine as long as they continue to live, he is going to teach someone the way he made the medicine."

You understand, all of these animals contributed meat taken from their hearts, not their thighs, as others say. And this is the first time that the Senecas obtained that Little Water medicine. [Other sources insist that the sacred powder is composed of meat cut from the thighs of living animals, who were released, healed themselves, and survived.]

When the hunter returned home, he taught the people to sing the songs that he had in his mind. Then he taught them what they must obtain to make the medicine.

That is the best medicine on earth.

[Here Chauncey tied up the legend until another time. He later continued as follows.]

And so now his tutelary animal instructor appeared to the hunter a third time during his sleep.[15] He said, "I shall instruct you further about the other kind of medicine." The hunter agreed. "I shall tell you what it says in the songs [the meaning of the song texts]. Some day you will need to make some more medicine, which will be nearly as effective as the first one that I taught you."

"All right, tell me."

His familiar told him, "You must mix the roots of some herbs. There will be a song that relates of the medicine." The first period of songs relates the search for the herbs. Swamp saxifrage [*ʔoi:yenʔ, Saxifraga pennsylvanica* L.] is the only herb specifically mentioned in the song texts.

Earlier Versions

The legend of the Good Hunter that I had from John Jimerson and Chauncey Johnny John has a long history among the Senecas, and it is even reported from Wyandot sources (Beauchamp 1901). The earliest Seneca version, collected by Eben N. Horsford at mid-nineteenth century, which appears in Lockwood Doty's *History of Livingston County, New York* (1876), repeats elements and incidents reported by

---

15. Again, the story follows the pattern of Seneca origin legends.

Element	Clarke 1870	Johnson 1881, after Myrtle 1855	O'Bail 1885	Parker 1908	John Jimerson	Chauncey Johnny John
Good Hunter	x	x	Bloody Hand	x	x	x
Scalped	x	x	x	x	x	x
Cherokees	x	x	x	x	x	x
Victim returns unrecognized	x				x	x
Council of animals	x	x	x	x	x	x
Conductor	Eagle	Bear-Eagle	Raven	Bear	Panther	Panther
Retriever	Pigeon Hawk	Crow	Black Hawk	x	Crow fails, Raven + Crow	x
Mystic animals make medicine	x	x	x	x	x	x
Power of song		x	x	x	x	x
Sing four times		x	x	x	x	x
Song taboo		x	x	x	x	x
Transformation					x	x
Dream revelation						x
Relates cure			x	x	x	x
Founds society		x	x	x	x	x
War bundle		x	x	x	x	x

FIGURE 3. Comparison of six versions of the legend of Good Hunter.

my sources. Instead of Crow or Raven, Pigeon Hawk retrieves the scalp from the Cherokee village.[16]

Even greater detail, surprisingly, occurs in the version of Elias Johnson (1881), a Tuscarora chief, who ascribed the legend to his own people although he cribbed it from a Seneca source (Barbara Graymont, personal communication 1999). Fox discovers the body and gives the death cry; animal and bird moieties fail to revive the hunter; Crow succeeds in fetching the scalp; Dew Eagle moistens it; customary water-scrying is described; and later a song heard leads the hunter to the plant, which regenerates itself after providing a generic alternative to the animal medicine. Johnson even described the ceremony for renewing the medicine twice a year—at the hunting season and in the spring when the deer changes coats. Johnson was a notable copyist, and I find no evidence that the Tuscaroras shared the complex with the neighboring Senecas.

The Wyandot version of Peter D. Clarke (1870) belongs in the same genre. It conforms closely to the Jimerson and Johnny John versions (see fig. 3): Good Hunter and carrion eaters; the role of Eagle; Hawk retrieves scalp; duck-bill spoon for administering the medicine; patient hears song, animals reply *yo hee:;* spirit transformation; hunter returns home unrecognized; hunter revived and repatriated.

Solomon O'Bail of Cattaraugus, a descendant of Cornplanter, in 1885 related the legend of "Bloody Hand" to Jeremiah Curtin (Curtin and Hewitt 1918: 273–79), which version is clearly the ancestor to the versions of John Jimerson and Chauncey Johnny John. It contains all of the elements found in the versions I collected, besides several unique elements.

In O'Bail's version, Bloody Hand, the good hunter, bears the same relation to the raptors. Black Hawk, not Raven, retrieves the scalp. Blood obtained from the magic cornstalk and magic squash seed combine with the flesh of animals to compound the medicine.

---

16. Passenger pigeons were still extant at the mid-nineteenth century (Fenton and Deardorff 1943).

Chickadee delivers medicine by mouth to the patient's stomach. The taboo on singing the songs out of ritual context and the proscription that the singer must hold the medicine occur for the first time. Just then some twenty men at Cattaraugus held packets of the medicine.

Notes on administering the medicine and renewing it follow (Curtin and Hewitt 1918: 491–92). Spotting the medicine in cardinal directions vis-à-vis the patient, in water dipped with the stream, preceded water scrying. If medicine and water fail to mix, the patient will die; if the medicine dissolves and the water remains clear, the patient will live. The patient drinks the clear concoction. White beans, white corn, and so forth promote health; avoid colored foods. Seclusion ensures that the patient will not see a passing mourner who has viewed a corpse. The patient swallows the medicine at first song of the curing rite.

Curtin's notes (Curtin and Hewitt 1918: 491–92) clarify the song texts for Groups I and II of the renewal ceremony, which replicates making the medicine:

Group I
1. I have been to the place where the plant grows.
2. I have been to the mountain [not the village].
3. I have been to the waterfall.
4. I have been beyond the clouds.

Group II
1. We meet where the tobacco is.
2. Now we are met, say the ducks.
3. Now we are met, says the two-prong deer.
[Further songs in each group are not specified.]

In a manuscript notebook collected by Joseph Keppler at Cattaraugus and accessioned into the Huntington Free Library in the hand of George G. Heye in 1925, John Jacket, an alleged descendant of Red Jacket, wrote out the song texts of *gano:daʔ,* dating the manuscript November 3, 1845 (ms. p. 3). The date "Feb 1871" appears on the fourth page of the song text, along with the name Joshua Pierce, who apparently wrote what follows in a different hand. The original hand returns for the first two songs opening the third period, after which Joshua Pierce resumes to the end (song texts, pp. 5–8).

The songs are grouped in four periods, and they number 92, which compares favorably with versions sung at Cattaraugus and Allegany until recently. Their content is much the same. They are grouped in pairs as follows: Group I, 12 pairs; Group II, 12 pairs; Group III, 16 pairs; Group IV, 6 pairs. But each song line is marked to be sung twice, as is its paired response, and the pairs in each group are numbered (as above), the 46 pairs becoming 92 song lines.[17]

The two-part version of Edward Cornplanter (Parker 1908: 150–56) derives from John Jacket and belongs to the same genre as the versions of John Jimerson and Chauncey Johnny John, but it is more satisfactory in explaining the origin of both the medicine and *i:ʔdo:s*. Night birds discover the fallen Good Hunter and notify the raptors. Wolf comes upon the body and summons the animals, who decide to restore him, for a living man must have a scalp. Crow fails in his mission to recover the scalp, but Pigeon Hawk recovers it. Bear oversees the cure and requickening. The therapeutic power of the song and dance of the mystic animals is replicated in *i:ʔdo:s*. The all-night sing finds its counterpart in the sessions to renew the medicine.

---

17. Publication of this notebook manuscript has been deferred pending further research with Professor Wallace Chafe.

⬥ 3 ⬥

Renewing the Medicine

Repeated observations of the all-night ceremony to renew the strength of the Little Water medicine in three Seneca communities and interviews with key participants enabled me to establish the sequence that governs its performance. In this chapter I treat the song cycles at Allegany and Tonawanda and discuss local variations that are either attacked or defended by singers who strive to get it right. Although I present my observations in the present tense, as I originally wrote them, the time referred to is the 1930s and 1940s.

The Little Water Society meets three times a year at Allegany and Cattaraugus Reservations to renew the strength of the medicine. At Tonawanda, in recent years, it meets but twice—according to Simeon Sky, in the spring, "when the deer sheds his coat," and in the winter, "when he renews it"—unless a death follows the use of the medicine, which renders the medicine inactive until renewed. Then the society meets at midwinter.

The ceremony of renewal is called ʔondiyenʔgwaʔyeons or, more commonly, hadiyenʔgwaʔye:ni, "they set tobacco down for it," which refers to setting a dish of tobacco on the floor for smokers. At Tonawanda, where the ceremony is more elaborate, the headman sets down eight pinches of tobacco, paired in eight rows, male and female, on a white cloth adjacent to the bundle, to represent the four periods of singing. He picks these up in counterclockwise rotation at the close of singing and puts the tobacco away until the next meeting. At Allegany (Coldspring) and Cattaraugus (Newtown), the first and great feast of renewal falls two days before the full moon of Green Corn; the winter meeting occurs on the fifth night of the new moon of *ni:skowakneh,* which is the night following the "great ceremonial mark" (*kaiwanonskwa?go:wa*), the so-called Feast of Dreams.

When the Berry Moon is new (in its first phase) and strawberries are in season, the third renewal of the medicine occurs.

Unique to society members at Tonawanda is a fifth canto of songs that they call the "Seneca group," which they insert as a fourth group at the autumn sing.

Ritual Pattern

The rites of the Little Water Society conform to a pattern shared with other Iroquois medicine ceremonies. A headman or conductor appointed for the occasion invites the members and enlists the singers. A meeting agenda encompasses a general thanksgiving, a tobacco invocation specific to the occasion, singing of the proper ritual songs, thanking the participants, and sharing the terminal feast. At Newtown on the Cattaraugus Reservation, the two leaders of the society should be of opposite moieties, and each leader has a young man as a servant. At Coldspring on the Allegany Reservation, however, a single head bundle holder manages the society and directs the ceremonies of renewal. He collects each member's contribution of tobacco on arrival, arranges the seating, seats the members, lays out the bundles and ritual paraphernalia, directs the ceremony, passes the berry water at intermissions, and apportions the terminal feast.

During the 1930s and 1940s at Coldspring, a typical renewal had these parts:

1. Seating and arrangements by headman
2. Thanksgiving address by appointed speaker

3. Laying out bundles and ritual tools
4. Tobacco invocation by appointed priest
5. Smoking and passing berry juice
6. Period I: lights out, whistle sounds, leader raises the songs of Group I
7. Intermission: light comes on, members smoke, pass berry juice
8. Period II: lights out, whistle sounds, singer raises the songs of Group II
9. Second intermission: as above
10. Period III: same routine
11. Third intermission: same routine
12. Period IV: same routine
13. Light comes on: headman collects rattles, puts away medicine; participants smoke, finish berry juice, and anticipate the feast
14. Terminal speech thanking participants
15. The feast: headman passes pig's head and ladles corn soup into members' pails
16. Members "scatter and fly in all directions" (carry corn soup home)

The Song Cycle

For Iroquois singers, the songs of the Little Water Society assume the character of chamber music. They sometimes refer to this singing as *kano:taʔ*. From the introductory antiphonal, the whistle imitating the eagles in flight, and the cries of the mystic animals, the songs progress through the first movement, recounting the search for the medicine, to the cries announcing animals who cured the Good Hunter, the mention of sacred places, and the recovery of the scalped hunter. The four cantos comprise a quartet that in thematic treatment approaches a native symphony. One notices a gradual increase of the beat; vibrato intensifies between songs; paired male and female songs reply in antiphony; and pitch rises toward the end.

One Coldspring version that John Jimerson learned at Cattaraugus in his youth has 96 songs: 18 in Group I, 20 in Group II, 40 in Group III, and 18 in Group IV. He insisted, "There will never be any more; there will never be less. Always the same." Jimerson recounted how he learned the songs:

Two of us decided to learn the songs, since frequently singers were scarce at the meetings three times a year. There was a vacant log house on my place on Plank Road. Ward Snow agreed to come there and teach us candidates the songs.

I got the place ready, swept out the log house, and they came at night. The two other candidates, besides myself, had frequently sat among the other Little Water singers. I thought the songs would be difficult to learn.

First, the instructor burned tobacco, telling the medicine what he was up to. Then we sat about gossiping and smoking. (I had prepared berry juice and a pail of white beans and sugar, but no corn soup or feast, as this was only a practice session.) Next he [Snow] spread kernels of corn on the table in four parallel rows, one row for the old woman, and one for the man. Each kernel represented a song.

The instructor or his assistant would tell me the name of the song and what animal it stood for. "Now," he said, "someone try to sing them." The other two candidates were older than I was and had heard the songs many times, but they were unable to learn them. Then I tried the woman's songs. Singing the man's part is easy, for it repeats, changing the gender. When I had finished the first group, I said, "How is that?" The instructors answered, "All right."

So I started the second group and went through to the end. Once more I asked, "How was that?" And again he replied, "All right."

Then I went through the third group, which has the most songs. I went through that too all right, and again asked, "How was that?" And again Ward Snow replied, "All right."

The last group of songs is easiest, and they are not so many. Group four, however, reaches the highest pitch. The

other night [referring to the meeting at Newtown that he and
I had attended on August 24, 1934] I nearly cried singing up
there.

John added that Sonon?gai:s ("Long horns"), or James Crow of the
Deer clan, had tried his best to reach way up there and, unable to
make it, had broken the flute in frustration.[1] On another occasion
John confessed that he never felt comfortable as lead singer for the
second group.

In the late 1930s and early 1940s, when I was most active in
fieldwork and regularly attended the renewals at Coldspring, Chauncey
Johnny John guided me on such matters. He became the active song
holder after John Jimerson's death. Chauncey seated me beside him
among the singers to make certain that I learned the songs properly.
The arrangement became a learning experience—not to bump my
feet with the cadence, to hear the rhythm, and to memorize the tag
lines as the leader lined out the song and as his partner, the second
singer, followed with the mate to it. Gradually, the din of the gourd
rattles in the flourishes creates an effect of overtones, as if the song
were coming from beneath the benches. No wonder people say they
hear women's voices. The cries of birds and animals—a crow, a fox
barking, an owl hooting, a wolf howling along the rim of the valley—are all real enough. At one winter meeting during subzero tem-
peratures, the house suddenly contracted with the boom of a cannon.
The singers stopped, people muttered, and the conductor went to
the fire and burned tobacco. It was the sort of omen that no one
present wanted to discuss.

In the summer of 1938, Chauncey dictated and explained the
texts of 98 songs that he regularly sang for the renewal ceremony
(Field Notes 1938, Fenton Papers, APS Library). He later recorded
the whole cycle for the Library of Congress: Group I, 22 songs;
Group II, 22; Group III, 42; and Group IV, 12.

---

1. The Little Water flute is merely a whistle, having no holes and stops for the fingers. It is called *ga:?genda?*.

The eleven paired songs of the first group—the first in each pair representing a woman speaking, and its partner, the reply by a man—recount stations in the search for the medicine. The woman's voice is going there; the man's voice has been to that place—to a hill (where the sacred cornstalk grows); to the fields; to the end of the fields; to the wood's edge and into the forest; to the swamp; to a place where saxifrage grows; to a little spring where animals go to drink; to a waterfall; to a windfall; to a lightning-struck tree; back to the hill to its top; back to where one started; back beyond the flying clouds (a reference to Dew Eagle, who came down to participate in curing the Good Hunter). Chauncey remarked that he hated to sing this group because he no longer held the medicine.

The eleven paired verses of the second period describe the arrival of members with tobacco at the meeting; then they name the mystic animals who have come. A duck calls; another species of duck named *sosogi:* is heard; it is followed by a large water bird with webbed feet that eats carrion, named *dyehdo:gen?,* and by another called *dadawine?* that is wheeling in flight. And Big Raven settles down to alight, ending the period.

Period III, which is sung only at the autumn renewal, the big meeting, comprises twenty-one pairs of songs. It opens with some-one about to go to sleep. The singer hears a female and a male owl hooting afar. An animal passed and left a track in the moss. An animal passed this way along the creek (presumably a doe and buck deer). She gives him something; he gives her something. A pretty blossom she gives him; he reciprocates. Yonder blossom she gives him; he reciprocates. Two females go to the creek (go to water). They both go there. She swims; he swims. She shows above water; he shows above water. Both female and male animals protrude above water. (Chauncey knew no meaning for this twelfth pair.) Pairs 13 and 14 address the handsome Raven, who has a pretty face. Pair 15: her face is close (as in whispering); his face is close. She likes to go in the water; he does too. They gather near the creek. Where she goes no one knows; him either. Pair 19: wherever unknown. Female crow

(Raven) wheels in flight; the male crow circles. Pair 21: the female alights; the male does likewise (to end that period).

The fourth period at the big autumn sing—otherwise the third period at midwinter and the Berry Moon—comprises six pairs of songs. It opens with female crow (Raven) taking off, as does the male. Nonsense vocables (*yowine*) dominate the second pair. A male sings the next two pairs. In song 5 he says: "My arm hangs limp"; in song 6, "My arm is cut at the biceps"; and in 7, "Blood runs down my arm." Song 8 consists of references to the Good Hunter; I am uncertain of the words. The fifth and sixth pairs return to the female-male alternation. In song 5, "She wheels in flight; he soars." In 6, "Female crow (Raven) alights; male crow alights; they both come to a stop, both crows (ravens)."

Chauncey remarked, "This is the end when they both sit down. This is *gahga?go:wa:*'s song."

Chauncey further commented that of the three meetings—those at *niskowakne, oyaikne,* and *gende?onkneh* (midwinter, Berry Moon, and Green Corn)—the last is the great meeting when they use all of the songs—all four groups. Autumn is the season when the animals grow new coats, when they fix the medicine. It is also the season for gathering herbs, after the stalks wilt and the strength returns to the roots. Autumn is the season for mixing medicines. The second group of songs is omitted at the other two meetings. They do not use all of the songs at midwinter (when animals are hibernating and roots and herbs are sleeping).

Chauncey had told me previously that he had learned the foregoing songs from his father at Cattaraugus, but when I asked him in 1938 whether they were the Cattaraugus version of the songs, he said, "No, mine are the old Coldspring songs that Haowan?go:wa:, Alice White's great-grandfather, sang. Alice's mother taught them to me. She used to come to our place every spring when we lived at Quaker Bridge because she liked [to listen to] spring frogs. While visiting us she taught me both *hadiyen?gwa?ye:ni* and *i:?do:s.* Women do know the songs: Alice White knows them. Last fall when I sang for the fall meeting at Hiram Watt's place, she said at the end, 'You are all right' [meaning that Chauncey had sung the version she preferred]."

In 1942, Alice White denied that her mother had taught the songs to Chauncey. She confirmed that her mother had learned the songs from her father, Captain Isaac, or Haowan?go:wa:, who was a great singer, but said she had taught the songs to her husband, not to Chauncey. "He must be mixed up."

Variations at Tonawanda

Simeon Sky (Dzokdeowa:?, Big root), the lead singer at Tonawanda in the mid-1930s, was sightless and had been trained as a piano tuner in a school for the blind. He was gifted with absolute pitch and a prodigious memory. Simeon believed that the medicine had chosen him to sustain its songs. He said, "I sing the songs, but frequently I do not understand their meaning. When I learned them, and during later rehearsals, for which they burned tobacco, an older member might recite the origin legend, but there was no song-by-song explanation.

"I refused to sing three times, but the old people said that I must have been selected by the medicine to be their song holder, although my voice is not really suited to the range of songs. In spite of myself, I learned the first two periods on the first night of rehearsal. The third period gives me the greatest trouble. And so I learned them all."

Aware that I had been admitted to the renewal rites at Coldspring and that I would probably attend upcoming rites at Tonawanda, Simeon proceeded to enlighten me on what differences to expect.

The Tonawanda version of the renewal ceremony comprises 62 songs, each of which is sung twice (in female and male counterparts), making 124 songs in five groups: Group I, 10 songs (20 pairs); Group II, 16 (32); Group III, 15 (30); Group IV, 8 (16); Group V, 13 (26).

As at Coldspring, Group I describes the search for the medicine, and Group II, the meeting of the medicine animals, their arrival, where they meet, and how they sing together. Period III treats of places, the council of animals,[2] the fates of birds who searched for Good Hunter's scalp, how one was killed, and how *gahga?go:wa:* (Big Crow or Raven) finally snatched the scalp from the smoke hole of a Cherokee lodge.[3] It is the most difficult group to sing. Period IV is composed of eight short songs, as at Coldspring. So much is sung at the spring meeting. Period V, the so-called Seneca group, is unique to Tonawanda; it is sung only at the autumn meeting, when it is inserted as a fourth group following Period III. It contains some of the same songs found in Period III of the Coldspring version and perhaps that of Newtown, although Jesse Cornplanter, a Newtown native living at Tonawanda, experienced difficulty with some of the Tonawanda songs. The Seneca group describes where the mystic animals meet, how two animals go to a stream (go to water); how two big crows are sitting in a meadow; and how they are dancing in a clearing.

Participant Observation

During the 1930s and 1940s, I witnessed the renewal ceremony repeatedly in the three Seneca communities in western New York: Newtown on the Cattaraugus Reservation (September 1934); Coldspring on the Allegany Reservation (September 1938, January 1939, 1956?, etc.); and Tonawanda (September 1935, October 1936, and with Edmund Wilson in June 1959). Observation complements informant testimony and affords leads for further inquiry, whereas native sources tend to stress elements of significant behavior that compose the ritual pattern and prepare the ethnologist to observe

---

2. According to Chief Solon Sky, the Tonawanda version holds that the council of animals came to one mind, except for Turkey Buzzard (*jenhdo:gen?*), who said, "I want him [the fallen hunter] to get real ripe and then he will be good eating." Turkey Buzzard was the lone dissenter.

3. When the council of animals charged a certain bird to go fetch the fallen man's scalp, that bird went but never returned. The fifth song of Group III, according to Simeon, relates how the bird went on the mission and was killed.

intelligently. Much else goes on that is incidental and reflects the impact of participating personalities who shape the occasion.

In the first winter of my fieldwork at Coldspring I did not presume to attend the session of the Little Water Society, nor was I invited. Myron Turkey, husband of the matron of my adoptive family, next day described the proceedings for me: "On entering the meeting, one puts a packet of tobacco in the twined corn-husk dish, and its contents go into the fire during the tobacco invocation or are later smoked by the members."

He listed members attending, distinguishing holders of the medicine, who bring their packets. The headman joins these with the main bundle during the renewal. One woman brought a packet of medicine but sat apart while other women sat in an adjoining room.

The headman spreads a folded white sheet (anciently white buckskin) on the floor and sets the main bundle on it. On a signal, holders surround the main bundle with individual packets, which must be down there during the tobacco invocation.

Members bring a gourd, squash, or pumpkin rattle to the meeting and place it beside the medicine bundle, to retrieve it after the invocation. The headman, with advice from the lead singer, seats the participants in groups. Members converse and smoke until the lights go out.

The two headmen who conduct the meeting should be of opposite moieties, and they may double as first and second singers, or Ravens (*gahga?go:wa:*).

Altogether, Myron outlined the ritual pattern substantially as I summarized it earlier in this chapter.

The Little Water Society at Tonawanda (1935–37, 1959)

Following my two seasons of fieldwork at Coldspring (Allegany), the U.S. Indian Service enabled me to spend two and a half years in almost daily contact with the Tonawanda Band of Senecas. The Little Water Society flourished "down below" among the Longhouse people, who invited me to sit in the renewal ceremony on at least two occasions for which I have notes. Again, in 1959, Edmund Wilson and I shared a session (Fenton 1991; Wilson 1959).

As previously noted, Simeon Sky, the lead singer, served as my mentor. In his role as lead singer, he held one of the medicine company's gourd rattles, which a former member had passed on to him shortly before his death.

Two members of the Turtle clan held the only bundles of the medicine then remaining at Tonawanda. One, held by a sachem, was regarded as the principal bundle, from which they took medicine for curing. It was composed of older packets formerly held by individuals.

The Tonawanda version of the renewal ceremony differs, my mentor pointed out, from the versions sung at Coldspring (Allegany) and at Newtown (Cattaraugus), which are nearly alike.

Simeon said, "We have a group of songs which the other two [Seneca] reservations do not know. We sing them at the fall meeting, when the deer sheds his coat and renews it for winter. We meet again in the spring, when the animals shed their winter coats." This was the old way. During the 1930s there had been three meetings, the third at midwinter.

At Tonawanda, anyone who belongs to *i:ʔdo:s* is considered a member of the medicine company: he is *hotcinohgenʔ*. He automatically belongs to the Little Water Society. When a person takes the Little Water medicine, even though he is subsequently released, he still belongs to the "medicine animals' society," the so-called *honontcinohgenʔ*. Simeon reasoned, however, that even though he took the Little Water medicine and it was released after the proper interval of four days with the proper ceremony of release (*sa:wennonʔtga:ʔ*), which is a form of *i:ʔdo:s*, (logically) he was freed of membership obligations. "Even though I sing, you cannot say that I belong to the Little Water Society. But if they had prescribed *i:ʔdo:s* for my cure, instead of releasing the medicine which I took, then I would belong to *honontcinohgenʔ* [the medicine society]."

Simeon added that the men who hold the bundles are of exemplary character. They stand in a special relation to the medicine and to the society of mystic animals who comprise the Little Water membership. In the ceremony of singing to renew the strength of the medicine (*hadiyen?gwa?ye:ni*), bundle holders, in taking the dipper of berry juice that is passed to them, address the mystic animals, who make up the society of meat eaters, saying, "Otgwanon:yon? swatcinonhgen?shon? [We return thanks (greet) you of the medicine society]."

Others, who do not hold bundles but merely have been cured, should not make the mistake of saying this line—which nevertheless they frequently do—but should say, "Otgwanon:nyon? dwaso:t [I return thanks to our grandfather]."

It is the headman's duty, before the ceremony begins, to instruct the bundle holders and other members and nonmembers in what they should properly say when invoking their helpers.

The autumn meeting of the Little Water Society at Tonawanda, held on October 19, 1935, was the second meeting that I attended and the first that I annotated. Simeon Sky and Corbett Sundown sponsored me. The floor plan and arrangement of those in attendance are shown in figure 4. The large square on the left side of the room indicates the table on which were arranged the eight pinches of tobacco (later put away with the medicine until the next sing), the lamp (which is turned down during intermission), the two medicine bundles, the dish of tobacco, and the five "flutes" (two whistles, three flageolets). Women, children, and nonsingers sat in the adjoining room on the right, and the feast was stored on the stairway (bottom of diagram) at the rear of house. The numbers around the left side correspond to the names of the participants in the following list.

1. Emerson Infant (Ga?nogai:?, Turtle clan): keeper of bundles, speaker, tobacco invocation, lamp tender
2. Corbett Sundown (Hawk clan): keeper of society's rattles, ritual conductor, doorkeeper
3. Simeon Sky, age 64 (Dzokdeowa:?, "Big root," Turtle clan): first song holder, whistle blower; arranged song periods and rested with (2)

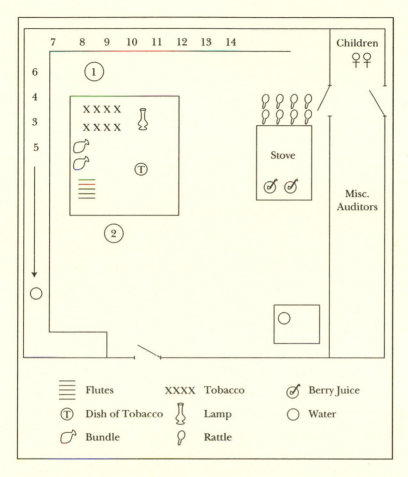

FIGURE 4. Floor plan and seating arrangement for the renewal
ceremony at Tonawanda, 1935.

4. Sylvester Ground, age about 30 (Deer clan): second song
   holder; has nearly mastered songs
5. Herman Jones, age about 35: helper to (3), learning songs
6. Felzie Scrogg, age 30: helper to (4); learner
7. Harrison Ground (Turtle clan): other doorkeeper
8. Yankee Spring (Beaver clan): sometime bundle holder
9. Onondaga or Cayuga from Canada (Six Nations)

10. Variously, Garfield George, Eugene Smith, etc.
11. Jesse Cornplanter (Snipe clan): member of Newtown lodge
12. Benjamin Hill, a strong singer
13. Lyman Blackchief
14. Unknown

Distinctive Features of the Little Water Ritual at Tonawanda

A strong moiety tradition prevails at Tonawanda in terms of the complementary roles of singers, conductors, and doorkeepers. As Elijah David (Hawk clan) put it, "One singer sings the part of 'our grandfather' [*sedwaso:t*]; his partner sings for 'our grandmother' [*etiso:t*]."

A distinctive arrangement of ritual paraphernalia also obtains: medicine bundles placed on table covered with white muslin; lamp kept in room instead of being carried out each period by the doorkeeper; two packets of medicine kept covered with white cloth; eight pinches of tobacco laid out in counterclockwise sequence by the bundle holder:

$$8 \quad 7 \quad 6 \quad 5$$
$$1 \quad 2 \quad 3 \quad 4$$

Same later picked up in sequence and put away with bundle until the next periodic sing. A set of five flageolets pertain to the society's bundle, of which two are whistles and three have three finger stops. These are sounded at the beginning and end of each period.

Five periods of songs are sung at the autumn meeting. The fourth group is inserted between the usual third and fourth periods.

The 1935 autumn sing adhered to these times:

11:00–11:30 P.M.:	opening invocations
11:30 P.M.–12:20 A.M.:	Period I, a single melody
1:00–1:25 A.M.:	Period II, a single melody until final songs
2:00 A.M.–3:15 P.M.:	Period III, increasingly higher pitch

4:00–4:20 A.M.:	Period IV, inserted "Seneca" group
5:00–5:20 A.M.:	Period V (otherwise fourth group)
5:20–5:45 A.M.:	Final speech, thanks, feast, and departure

Soon after the session, Corbett Sundown (Hawk clan), who conducted the ceremony, explained his role and that of his opposite, Harrison Ground (Turtle clan). The bundle holders notify these two men whenever they wish to hold a meeting.

The medicine holders (*haden:net*) were then Emerson Infant and Paddy Ground, both of the Turtle clan. Literally, "they take care"; they are "keepers." If anyone gets hurt and needs to notify them, either one may administer the medicine.

In 1935, Corbett Sundown had served as messenger and ritual holder for fourteen years. He was still active in that role some twenty-four years later (Wilson 1959: 290ff.). His membership in the medicine society dated from early childhood. In his words:

When I was a kid, I got sick and nearly died. I was in a coma for nearly a week. My grandfather, Charley Bigfire, veteran of the First World War, lived next door. He was a clairvoyant [*daya?dowewetha?*], able to divine things in his dreams. He came here and told my mother that I had but one more day to live. He held my hand when I came to; the doctors had given up on me. He placed in my hand something I could not make out, and he asked me whether I could tell what he had placed in my hand. Finally he told me that it was an ear of white corn, which I could not make out. He said, "This will keep you for the day. I am going for the hog's head, and you shall have *hon-ontcinohgen?* [the medicine company]." He left the ear of corn as a token, as a protector. When they made the corn soup for the ceremony, that ear of corn went into it. He told my mother that if she did not hurry, I would not live that day.

The next night I awoke [regained consciousness] to hear the first song of *honontcinohgen?*, the members of the medicine company, singing the opening song of *hadi:?do:s,* or *i:?do:s.* I knew from where I was in the bedroom that there was a great crowd sitting about the kitchen singing. After the ceremony was over they went home. I felt better and was soon able to walk around a year later.

Chief Edward Black (also Hawk clan) was in charge of the renewal ceremony at that time. He gave it up, and they appointed me to succeed him. At that time Charlie Ground (Bear clan) was servant for the other moiety.

Harrison Ground was appointed later. Between renewal ceremonies, as part of his duties, Corbett acted as keeper of the society's rattles, a role that has no title. Charlie Ground previously kept the rattles.

The medicine society at Tonawanda met twice in 1935, but in years when someone who used the medicine died, the society held a third winter meeting on the first Saturday (about five days) after the new moon of *niskowakneh,* but not on the eve of the Indian New Year (Midwinter Festival). In June, the society met on the first Saturday following the new moon of *o:yaikneh,* the Berry Moon. The fall meeting was held on the first Saturday after the moon of *ge:onkneh* (late August–early September). "This year [1935] we got it wrong because Emerson Infant, the principal bundle holder, at the June meeting mispronounced *ge:onkneh* and said *gahsaʔkhneh,* which falls in late October or November."

A year later, on October 6, 1936, I met with Simeon Sky. He announced, "We are having the fall sing on October seventeenth." I asked Simeon whether the date had to do with the new moon (which fell on the fifteenth), two days before the meeting. He remarked, "We are now going by the old way—when the corn is in the strings— after the fall husking, when the husked corn is braided into strings and hung up to dry."

Corbett Sundown's Agenda

Chief Sundown's account of his duties as co-servant to the medicine society, although it repeats some items, affords an inside view of the ritual pattern.

First, the preliminaries. When the two bundle keepers think it time for the renewal, they confer, decide on the date, and notify the two servants, who make the preliminary arrangements. The two bundle keepers ask someone for the use of their house. (Nelly Clute's house had been the appointed place in recent years because it afforded room for the ceremony, excepting one year when the society met at Elijah David's place because Nelly's grandson had died.)

According to the old custom, no women who might be menstruating and no children were expected to attend. However, two women of opposite moieties—Sadie George (Turtle clan) and Abbie Gordon (Hawk clan)—served as cooks for the *hadiyen?gwa?ye:ni* (renewal ceremony). (Individuals do their own cooking for *i:?do:s,* personal renewals.) The two bundle holders donated the corn—one five quarts, the other a string.

Meanwhile, the two servants make the rounds notifying the members and collecting donations—a dime, a nickel, etc.

Next, the ritual pattern of the ceremony.

1. *Ganon:yonk,* general thanksgiving, followed by an explanation of the purpose of the meeting. Emerson Infant, principal bundle holder. (Corbett had appointed Henan Scrogg, a Snipe clan sachem, but he got drunk.) Chief Lyman Johnson (Wolf clan) used to serve as speaker and make the tobacco invocation.

2. Servant (Corbett) arranges ritual paraphernalia: white cloth on table, covers medicine bundle under cloth. (One is not supposed to open bundle or look at it; only keepers may see it. For as long as Corbett could remember, keepers mix the medicine packets together before the ritual, put it under the cloth, and separate it later.) Flutes and whistles laid beside it. Places rattles and feast food near the fire. Eight pinches of tobacco laid out as numbered in counterclockwise rotation:

$$8 \quad 7 \quad 6 \quad 5$$
$$1 \quad 2 \quad 3 \quad 4$$

In picking up the tobacco at the end of the singing, before the feast, one picks it up by twos: 1 and 8, 2 and 7, 3 and 6, 4 and 5. The tobacco goes with the medicine when the bundle is put away.

3. *Hayen?gontho:?,* the tobacco invocation.

4. Announcement by speaker. (Servants tell him what to say.) He instructs the head singers to take their seats, get things in order, and prepare for the servants to present them with rattles preparatory to singing.

5. Presentation of rattles. (Some members bring their own.)

6. First passing of berry juice (*?o:ya:gi?*). Servant announces: "Now we will drink the berry water." He presents the bucket, first to the bundle holders, second to the head singers. The two servants divide the room, each taking half, each presenting the dipper to a bundle holder, to one of the singers, and then to the remaining half of the room. (The seating is not according to moieties.)

7. One servant tells the other to put out the light. (Simeon Sky claimed that it was the old custom for the medicine keepers to tend the light.)

8. Period I. The ritual proper commences as soon as the lights go out. Simeon Sky starts to shake the rattle—two spaced downbeats, then gradual acceleration as the others join until they are in unison. The first singer cries *wi: yo;* the others respond: *wi: yo:.* Then, transposing, first singer: *yo: wih,* and the response: *yo: wih.*

As the tempo builds, the lead singer reaches for the flute and sounds three or four notes. Then he lines out the first song. Simeon, as first singer, invariably asks Corbett to sit next to him (as second singer). The first singer, having stated the text, depends on the second singer to carry the antiphonal, or the main body of the song.

Corbett remarked, "The first group of songs drag, and they take all of my breath."

◆4◆

The Anthropologist as Understudy

During the summer of 1938, after two and a half years at Tonawanda and a year of teaching at St. Lawrence University, I returned to Allegany to lead a field party of four students based in the Allegany School of Natural History in the adjacent state park. We enjoyed excellent rapport with the Coldspring Longhouse community. After my students departed, Chauncey Johnny John, then the lead singer, tutored me on the songs and procedures of the medicine society's renewal ceremony and promised to seat me beside him to learn the songs at its next meeting. Meeting my classes prevented my attending the autumn session, but Chauncey fulfilled his pledge at the winter meeting when I returned for the midwinter ceremonies.

The renewal ceremony is called *hadiyenʔgwaʔye:ni hadino:daiyaiʔ*, "they spread tobacco for the medicine song," although formerly people referred to it by the second word in that phrase, which refers to the sounding of the whistle (*gano:daʔ*).

Figure 5 displays the floor plan for the *hadiyenʔgwaʔye:ni* held at *niskowakneh* (moon of midwinter) in Coldspring on January 25, 1939. The ritual props were the medicine bundle, the tobacco, four gourd rattles, and three whistles. Participants were the following, numbered in correspondence to the seating arrangement shown in figure 5:

1. Sherman Redeye (Snipe clan): second singer
2. Chauncey Johnny John (Turtle clan): invoker, lead singer
3. Unknown
4. Hiram Watt (Deer clan): headman, whistle blower
5. Unknown
6. Henry Redeye (Bear clan): speaker
7. Unknown
8. Guest
9. Amos Johnny John (Wolf clan)
10. William N. Fenton (Hawk clan)
11. Aldrich Bill (Cayuga of Six Nations)

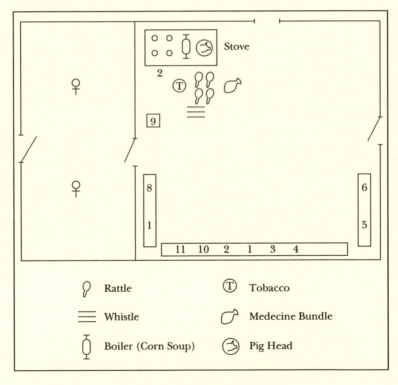

FIGURE 5. Floor plan and seating arrangement for the renewal
ceremony at Coldspring, 1939.

The ritual pattern consisted of the following events:

1. Seating the participants (headman)
2. Greeting and thanks (HR)
3. Arranging bundle, packets, ritual props, tobacco, and feast food near fire
4. Tobacco invocation (CJJ)
5. Members smoke, and first passing of berry juice (canned pears)
6. Lights out for Period I (whistle)
7. Intermission. Lights on. Smoke and second passing of berry juice
8. Period II
9. Intermission (as above)
10. Period III
11. Collect rattles and put away medicine (headman)
12. Finish berry juice
13. Speaker thanks participants
14. Feast: headman passes pig's head
15. Filling participants' pails with corn soup (headman)
16. Participants disperse, carrying pails home

Following are some observations of this meeting by M. Lismer, a member of my summer field school, who sat in an adjoining room:

> We arrived about ten P.M., but the ceremony did not begin until they all listened to the Joe Louis fight on the radio, which was mercifully short. Headman Hiram produced a bag of gourd rattles, and lead singer Chauncey brought others in a sack.
>
> Speaker Henry Redeye opened with the regular thanksgiving speech (*ganon:yonk*). Chauncey, standing at the stove, began the invocation, committing tobacco to the fire as he spoke. The headman passed the berry juice (canned pears), first to the men and then to the two women (bundle holders) sitting near them. One refused and the other took it. Door shut, lights off during the first period.

Intermission: lights on, smoke, and pass berry juice.

Period two, long series of songs.

Second intermission. High note of whistle represents bird call (Eagle).

Hot pork passed and remainder of juice. Finally, everyone put pails down on the kitchen floor, and headman apportioned boiler of corn soup in pails to take home.

Lismer interviewed the daughter of the headman next day:

The medicine that her father held was the only one that they regarded as "alive." During the singing one may hear a beautiful woman's voice, although there is no such woman present. It is the medicine doing that. Also, it causes the whistle lying on the floor to sound, although no one is near it.

Hiram's mother held the medicine, and he got it from her. It will pass to one of his children.

Women may sit with the singers. Big Geneva has done it twice. A woman would not likely sing, although she held a rattle.

Whenever a woman holding the medicine no longer wants to keep it, she may give it to another holding some of it. There is an appropriate transfer invocation.

For this occasion Dora Jimerson prepared the corn soup, although participation by women members (who had been cured by the medicine) in preparing the feast was not the old rule.

Parker (1908) implied that only men might cook. This may be the rule at Cattaraugus, as it is at Six Nations. The rule reflects the menstrual taboo. At Coldspring, in contrast with Canada (Six Nations) and anciently at Cattaraugus, where men were appointed to cook for the medicine society, older women were preparing the feast—hulled corn soup laced with kidney beans, and half a hog's head. It is considered permissible for women past menopause to cook, and for the same reason young women are discouraged. Older leaders appointed guards to prevent them from entering meetings. I observed such guards at Newtown and at Tonawanda.

Collaborators: Congdon and Deardorff

During the 1940s, two colleagues—the attorney Charles E. Congdon of Salamanca, New York, and Merle H. Deardorff of Warren, Pennsylvania—shared their observations at Coldspring with me, sometimes for meetings at which I was not present. Many of the Senecas of Allegany knew Congdon and had consulted him on personal matters as well as Seneca Nation affairs. They had adopted him and given him the name Haowan?go:wa:, "Big boat," of the Wolf clan, and he regularly attended major festivals at Coldspring Longhouse. Hiram Watt came to depend on Charlie to procure the hog's head for the renewal ceremony of the Little Water Society, which Charlie frequently attended. Merle Deardorff, a former school man and banker, was at heart a scholar and, like Charlie Congdon, was deeply committed to local history, which led him to the Senecas. He became a mentor to visiting ethnologists, including me. Deardorff was a generous man, and the Senecas loved him.

According to a memorandum that Charles Congdon wrote to me in January 1942, accidents befall the headman's kin for neglecting the medicine (see also Congdon 1967: 147–51). I summarize Congdon's memo as follows:

Hiram Watt, headman and bundle holder for the Little Water Society at Coldspring, neglected to hold a meeting to renew the medicine in the fall of 1941. He was preoccupied with the Six Nations meetings held annually for the preaching of Handsome Lake's message. Instead he went to Canada, where at Six Nations he sold some of the medicine for fifteen dollars. He failed to burn tobacco and sing some of the medicine songs for it. While he was there, a son cutting firewood over the river cut his foot. Then a grandson mangled a hand in the washing machine. While returning from the doctor's office in Salamanca, three of his kindred riding with him were killed when their vehicle met a truck head on—a daughter and two grandchildren. Other survivors were injured. True believers that the medicine must be sung for at least twice a year, and especially in the fall, maintained that Hiram's negligence of the medicine brought misfortune to his family.

In 1942, in my absence from Coldspring, Congdon procured the pig's head and arranged for Deardorff to attend the June (Berry Moon) meeting to renew the medicine, under the aegis of Chauncey Johnny John. A few items from Deardorff's notes are pertinent. His background in music came into play: "The 'flute', as played, produced only one fundamental tone, but by overblowing it emitted the octave above and the variation on both tones that can be made by embouchure. . . . During one intermission, Chauncey appeared to be showing one player more tricks than he apparently knew. The flute fluttered during Chauncey's solo parts. . . . The verses are all in antiphons. Chauncey sings the strophe (with flute and gourd rattle accompaniment); all come in on the antistrophe with gourds but no flute. Each verse ends in '*yenh!*' There is no harmony in the music, but the melody conforms to a pentatonic scale." Animal sounds appeared in the second period; most in the third: owl, crow, and cat. Others not identified.

At the first intermission, Chauncey called the headman's attention to the bowl of tobacco resting near the stove. The headman distributed this among the guests, who each had put in a paper or sack of tobacco on entering the meeting.

Following the meeting, Deardorff's friend Windsor Pierce of Cornplanter Grant came into the bank in Warren, Pennsylvania, where Deardorff had an office. After the usual miscellaneous talk, Windsor said, "I hear that you are going to this Little Medicine Society. You must look out for that. It is very dangerous." Windsor went on to tell how some people, when they want to get rid of someone, take that medicine and, with tobacco and a little whiskey, go somewhere where someone has been buried for six months and the ground has had a chance to steam. They dig down about two feet, dump the medicine in, and mention the person's name. "That fixes him. . . . I wouldn't get mixed up in that thing if I were you."

Congdon covered the June 1944 meeting to renew the medicine, although it is not clear that the medicine was present, Hiram Watt having sold some or all of it in Canada. If it was present, it remained in Hiram's big bag under the bench where he sat. Singers of opposite moieties sat facing each other on benches. Speakers of the complementary sides rendered thanksgiving and the tobacco invocation. Atkins Curry (Bear clan), whom Chauncey Johnny John had been training, led the songs in the female role, and Albert Jones (Snipe clan) replied in the male role. Group I, of 22 songs, lasted over an hour, Group II nearly an hour, and Group III somewhat less. The lead singer first lined out the song solo, then all repeated it together. The second singer then repeated the process with the mate to it. Between groups, intermissions with lights on were devoted to smoking and the headman's passing strawberry juice, after taking some himself. Individual thanks to the tutelaries were not reported. The feast afforded generous portions of hog's head and tasty corn soup laced with brown kidney beans. Chauncey remarked his pleasure at his pupil's singing.

The Society Goes Public

In 1946, after the death of Hiram Watt, who had conducted the affairs of the Little Water Society for many years and held the main bundle, the responsibility and the medicine bundle passed to Atkins Curry. Although Curry was not a Seneca by birth and had but a slight quantum of "Indian blood," he spoke Seneca and adhered to the Longhouse faith. He had mastered the repertoire of ceremonial songs, including the songs of the medicine society, which he had learned from Chauncey Johnny John. Under At Curry's regime, the society went public.

The first sign of change came on the third day of the Green Corn Dance, when Albert Jones announced that the fall meeting of the society would be held three days later at Atkins Curry's place, and everyone should understand that they were welcome to attend and contribute to the feast. He then passed a hat, going around the ceremonial circle to the right. I carried no money, but someone put in fifteen cents for me.

Previous meetings had been limited to bundle holders and conscripted singers, and they were held later in the fall. The announcement evoked some discussion in the community.

The following day, after the Great Bowl Game,[1] Chauncey brought up the subject of attendance at the medicine society meeting. Of course it was all right, he held, for adopted white men to come. I had told him that Merle Deardorff and I were hesitant until the leader of the society invited us. "Any member can invite you," he said.

That evening, as we returned from an ox roast at Steamburg, Clara Redeye asked me, "Are you going to the doings Wednesday? If you are, we want to go. Sherman [her husband] wants to sing. Anyone may go. You know the songs, and they will need you to help out if there are only a few singers." Albert Jones, himself a singer, confirmed this.

On the afternoon preceding the ceremony, Deardorff had a long talk with headman At Curry concerning the changes. Long at Hiram Watt's place, the meeting followed its new headman to his residence. Atkins said, "Hiram always had it too late. Only one date of the three annual meetings is fixed. A meeting must be held when the new moon [of midwinter] *djiskowakneh* is five nights old. Also a meeting must be held in the fall soon after *gende?onkhneh* [Green Corn], and a third after the Berry Moon [*?oyaikhneh*]. But there is no certain night for the latter two—just soon after the new moon. People have had different ideas about which moon is which; but now we are going to get things together and get back on schedule."

As for collecting in the longhouse to sustain the medicine: "We always take up a collection, but Hiram used to ask one of us to do it and told us to go only to those people who were interested. We think that the medicine is for all the people and that everyone ought to be given a chance to put in for it."[2]

---

1. The Great Bowl Game, one of the four sacred ceremonies, is played between the moieties at the Green Corn and Midwinter festivals (Fenton 1936).

2. Atkins told me the same day that Hiram had restricted the meetings for his own protection. He did not want people present who criticized his leadership or trusteeship of the medicine. He also let the members take their bundles home. Atkins disapproved of this for several reasons: "It is tribal medicine coming down from the old days of fighting with other tribes. It therefore belongs to all of the people. If it is out [in the community], it tends to be neglected, or worse, persons may wreak harm with it." He cited a specific example.

Atkins Curry told how he became headman of the Little Water Society:

> The man who holds the medicine must be a man of goodwill; he must not drink or hunt, for fear of offending the animals. There are not many here who could take that job. The people got together and sent Deforest Abrams [a longhouse officer] to ask me to take it. At first I said that I could not take it because the one who takes it must be ready to go anywhere at any time, at once, when someone calls for the medicine. He must also know the songs. Chauncey Johnny John and I are the only ones here who know them all. Moreover, I work on the railroad [in the section gang], and if I take off too much time, I might get in trouble. So I said I would not. They asked others but failed to get anyone to do it. Deforest then returned. He pointed out that I have over twenty years of service on the road and that no one could fire me without taking it clear up to the superintendent. He reasoned that I probably could take time off better than other men who have fewer rights. So I reluctantly agreed to do it.[3]

Atkins had been selected by "all the people," in his opinion, as well as the head longhouse officers. He intended to serve the community.

Deardorff pursued his inquiries: How much medicine remained? Atkins acknowledged having six or seven bundles. When called, he chose any one, regardless of who owned it. He used it sparingly that it might last a long time. He doubted that anyone living knew how to compound the medicine.

He held that anyone except children might attend meetings. "We don't like young people to come because they make fun of the medicine, mocking the songs and otherwise making trouble. Only persons who know how to sing to the medicine may enter the dark room. Others may listen outside."

---

3. Coldspring railroad workers having earned most rights comprised the "regular gang," while men with fewer rights made up the "extra gang." The regulars formed an elite group in Coldspring society during the 1930s and 1940s.

Atkins worried about persons having other bundles in the community. "They say people can do a lot of damage with that medicine . . . if so disposed." He wished it were all with him so that it could be used properly. "The song tells you. When you come to that place when treating a patient, it will say: 'Dip the water . . .' You do that. Without the song the medicine will do no good."

As the new headman of the Little Water Society, At Curry was taking his duties seriously. He had never expected to be chosen. Rather, he thought the office would fall to Chauncey Johnny John, his mentor, who knew most about it and with whom At had lived for ten years as a boy. Chauncey, however, seemed pleased with the people's selection and worked for At's success. Curry's first act was to procure a window shade to make a whistle to replace others that somehow had disappeared.

Having been assured that I would be welcome, I set about, with members of the Redeye household, to procure some Indian tobacco (*Nicotiana rustica*), or *oyen?gwa?on:weh*, to contribute for the invocation. Atkins Curry, who grew it, kindly obliged.

The 1946 Meeting

Members straggled in for an hour before the ceremony started. A wall and door separated the lodge (kitchen) from a somewhat larger other room, reserved for women and watchers (fig. 6). The headman had set eight o'clock as the time, hoping to get started at nine. Formerly, the doings started much later and broke up at dawn, but the work pattern set by the railroad had superseded older ceremonial patterns. Members of the "regular gang" and of the "extra gang" of track workers had succeeded an older generation who did not work at wage labor. Concepts of "work" and "time" dominated life. As the hour approached we were eight men with seven women in the adjoining room. I missed the old-timers who had gone the long trail. Chauncey and Albert represented them.

Albert Jones looked at his railroad watch and remarked to the headman, "This is the crowd. We had better get into it. We'll get done early and work tomorrow."

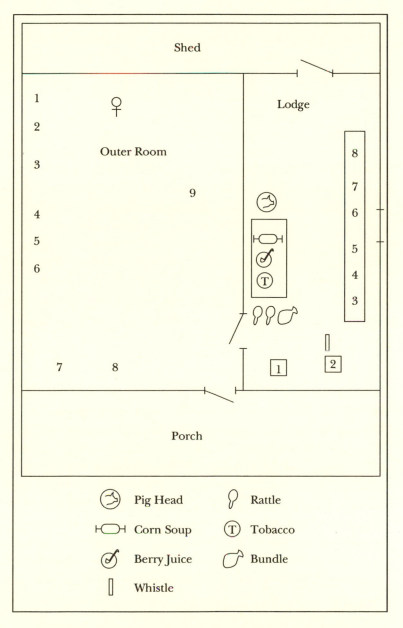

FIGURE 6. Floor plan and seating arrangement for the renewal
ceremony at Coldspring, 1946.

Headman seats the singers. This was an excellent opportunity to observe the role of the headman. At Curry appeared self-conscious about discharging his duties, which he took quite seriously. Equally interesting was to see how elders taught an appointed candidate to fulfill his office. The public had sanctioned At's appointment, and now the erstwhile ritual holder was coaching the new headman. Recall that Chauncey, a former bundle holder, had sheltered Atkins as a boy for ten years and taught him to perform ceremonial speeches and songs. In a sense, At was Chauncey's prodigy.

As headman and first singer, At (number 6 on the lodge side of fig. 6) had Deforest Abrams (7) and Sherman Redeye (8), both strong singers, on his right and Albert Jones (5), second singer and speaker, on his left. I (number 4) sat in a corner to allow a returned Navy veteran to sit next to the second singer to learn the songs—but Chauncey told At to switch us and seat me beside Albert, saying, "He knows some of the songs; he should learn all of it." I was put in the position of pupil, as I had observed other apprentices before me. As dean of the lodge, Chauncey (2) sat apart to listen with Jack Dowdy (1), who also knew the songs, or should have known them, having been there often enough, as Chauncey remarked. Albert would see to it that I heard the key words of the songs as they came up. Meanwhile, the headman instructed Albert what to announce.

The first and second singers were of opposite moieties, as were headman and speaker.

Opening address. Albert commenced his usual address of greeting and thanksgiving to the spirit-forces from earth to sky, which I had recorded for the Library of Congress at the first Conference on Iroquois Research the previous year. He went on to announce why the people had gathered. He declared this a meeting of the medicine company at the moon of *gendeʔonkneh* (Green Corn), which is the time that all four groups of songs are sung clear through to the end. He remarked on the succession of officers. All of the bundles had been brought together, so far as they knew. He remarked that the persons in the lodge numbered eight, but that seven (actually nine) sat in the outer room. He announced that Hauno?on (Chauncey) would make the tobacco offering, that At would lead the song, that Hanoje:nen?s (himself, in the third person) would assist, and that others would prop up the song. He mentioned that the rattles were lying there (beside the bundles), as was the whistle (*gano:da?*). Berry juice was provided to wash away the tobacco. There was a hog's head in lieu of bear, and hulled corn soup.

Headman arranges medicine bundles and ritual props. While Albert spoke, the headman, Atkins, arranged the bundles and brought out the ritual props. He set the bundles near the stove (fire) in a white market basket. I could neither count nor identify the individual packets, except that of Sarah Snow, old Gaji?jen?s, who came in late with her granddaughter. At produced rattles from a manila shopping bag and piled them beside the basket. Several rattles appeared to be quite old. I recognized a small crinoid squash rattle that Hiram Watt had formerly used. A dish on the drying-oven shelf held tobacco, to which the headman added contributions from individuals. (In the second group of songs, various birds enter bringing tobacco.) He checked the boiler of corn soup and the pan containing half a hog's head. The headman thought he had everything in order, but Chauncey reminded him that the whistle was not there. At disappeared and returned with it from upstairs, placing it so that it leaned on the basket of medicine. The stage was now set for the invocation.

Tobacco invocation. Chauncey, as on previous occasions, with dish of tobacco in hand, stepped to the stove, from which the headman lifted the lid and stirred the fire. A pinch at a time, he committed the tobacco to the flames. He addressed the tutelaries of the society on behalf of all the people. He thanked water, grasses, herbs, poles and trees, the medicine birds and animals. Near the end, however, he forgot to mention the names of the singers. When Atkins reminded him, it annoyed the old man. It was hot near the stove, and Chauncey was perspiring. He handed the dish to At and told him to go ahead and do it himself. At remarked to me later that Chauncey used to be a good speaker, but now he had to be watched lest he forget. It annoyed

Chauncey that his heretofore excellent memory was failing. So At put a patch on the invocation, something I had never seen before, asking the tutelaries to listen to him, who would lead the singing, and to Hanoje:nen?s (Albert Jones), who would assist.

First passing of berry juice and smoking. "Now, light up your pipes and smoke to our society," said the headman. Persons having pipes took tobacco from the dish that the headman passed. He handed a very short pipe to Chauncey, one that I had seen used previously in Dark Dance, or Bear Dance. Chauncey commented, "It is so short a person can smoke up his nose." This made a lot of fun.

When all had smoked some five minutes, the headman, with pail and dipper in hand, said, "This is to give thanks to your society and wash away the tobacco." As he passed the pail and dipper to a member, that person said, "I give thanks to your medicine society." One took as much as one pleased. The headman served himself last.

Period I. Pulling a light switch darkened the room, certainly handier than carrying a lamp into the other room. Both rooms were darkened, which was new. Nor were the shades drawn in the lodge, which enabled me to see the headman take his place as first singer, and Chauncey silhouetted against the moonlit windowpane, blowing the whistle. As the whistle fluctuated between octaves, singers, following the leader, shook rattles until they were in unison. Then came the cry *wi: yo:h wi: yo:h ya:h yo: wi:h yo: wi:h ya:h,* followed by the first song, "Here I go to the mountain, etc." The second singer responds, "I have been to the mountain."[4]

The time is four-four, with most of the notes held for four to eight beats. Thus I was able to anticipate and sing in time. Unless one knows the songs, the breathing is quite difficult. The first group of songs drags at a slow tempo that gradually quickens after the first pair of songs; but at that we dragged through the first two sets, when Sa?di:s (Fanny Stevens) shouted from the adjoining room to pick it

---

4. Contemporary ritualists interpret the root as "village," but older texts say "mountain," where the magic cornstalk grows.

up, and Chauncey admonished the first singer to get going. Then we improved and began to sing in unison.

Seated between the second singer and old Chauncey Johnny John, I enjoyed unique privileges. Albert, in his baritone voice, sang clearly, with fine quality. Occasionally he would whisper to me the keyword in the next song—"the old deserted village," "the windfall," "the lightning-struck tree"—so that I would recognize it when the leader lined it out.

The leader sings the song once completely; the company joins in on the repetition, and all then repeat it in unison. Each song is sung four times. Then follows the paired song in the same manner.

The period ends with the cries—*Yenh!* And the singers put their rattles down under the benches where they sit. Lights. Intermission: smoke and pass berry juice.

Period II. Opens with the same cries. The tune is different. The song summons the medicine animals to assemble and put down tobacco. It then proceeds to name those who attend, female and male, bringing tobacco. (The name of the ritual—*hadiyen?gwa?ye:ni,* "they put down tobacco"—derives from this. The speaker always mentions the names of those persons attending the meeting bringing tobacco.) Thus, the end of the eighth song says, "Gagwegon sahodiyei ne?ko hon:we gayen?gwa?yen?on [all have come here bringing tobacco]." Then the songs proceed to denominate those who have arrived. Songs 9 and 10 say, "A certain person has met at the place where the tobacco rests." Songs 11 and 12 say, "Here they sit down side by side." Then it names four waterbirds (a helldiver and three species of ducks); then the crow. Appropriate cries greet the announcement. The first four birds sit down side by side; crow and his kind wheel in flight, then alight. This ends the period, and another intermission follows.

Period III. This is the inserted period sung only once a year, when the deer changes its coat for the winter. It is the most demanding of the singer, for it has the greatest number of songs—twenty-one pairs, forty-two in all—and the pitch rises toward the end. (Chauncey recorded this as Period IV in his recording for the Library

of Congress.) It starts with the same introductory cries and ends
with the same concluding cries.

I recall this pair of songs: "She is going to sleep; he is going to
sleep." And toward the end, a streamside passage: "A mossy place, a
doe passed by; along the creek, she passed this way."

The entire period seems to follow the tracks of small deer—
female and male—to several places: "where the blossoms are," "they
go to the creek," "they swim," "their snouts protrude above water."
Then the song mentions the good looks of Big Crow, or Raven.

> They both like to go to the creek.
> They gather near the creek.
> Nobody knows where she goes.
> He goes around that way.
> Where have they gone?
> The Raven wheels in flight (female and male).
> Raven alights.

In this group, the songs go back to the beginning, to the signature,
where they end abruptly, with the rattles in vibrato.

Period IV. We were all relieved to reach the final period, which is
short, and more singers know the songs. The theme of the wounded
hunter predominates. The third and fourth pairs of songs are male:
"My arm hangs limp, blood runs down my arm" (see WNF field notes
1938 and 1941).

Collect rattles and put away medicine. We had put our rattles down
under the bench. The headman collected those rattles belonging to
the society. He passed berry juice and we finished it. Meanwhile, the
headman took the medicine out of the room and stashed it upstairs.
Just then I went out to get my camera in order to photograph the
feast, but I returned for the closing speech.

Terminal speech of thanksgiving and closing. The speaker went on at
great length to assure us that everything had been fulfilled by everyone, from the cooks on down: by headman, priest, speaker, singers,
those who helped, and those who came to listen. He hoped that

nothing might befall any of us returning home. He stated that the next meeting would fall on the fifth night of *niskowakneh*.

Feast. Passing of the hog's head and distribution of the corn soup. As a joke, Albert sent in the bone to his wife.

We scattered and flew in all directions.

The Bumping Feet Mystery

We had been interrupted toward the close of the singing by one of the women calling from the adjoining room. I thought it was because the lead singer had dropped a song. But someone among the listeners in the outer room had heard something. Apparently we had stopped singing to listen. Saʔdiːs said something, and after a pause to let the ring of the rattles die out in my ears, we had continued to the end.

When I returned from outside with my camera, Chauncey stood beside the stove offering tobacco to the fire. Then I sensed that something unforeseen had occurred. Sherman Redeye said to me, "The women heard something while we were singing. Someone's feet were bumping." Chauncey went on earnestly praying that nothing befall any of us. I noted visible concern on several faces.

Later, going home in the car, Clara and her daughter, Helen, burst out at once. "We both heard a noise like moccasined feet dancing. At first I thought it was someone bumping his feet—either a singer or one of the women listening. Geneva did not want us to say anything. She too had heard it, but she was wearing moccasins." The implication was that Geneva would not want anyone to think she was the one bumping her feet. I was sure that it had not been one of the singers, because we would have heard it first. The noise occurred twice.

Skepticism, mixed strangely with credulity, colored the remarks of Clara and her daughter. They seemed more convinced as time passed.

In a conversation with Lynn Dowdy the following day, he remarked on the incident of the dancing feet at the Little Water

Society meeting the previous night. The meeting had slipped his mind, and he had gone hunting upriver. Albert Jones had told him about the incident that day on the job at the Erie Railroad tracks—that while singing the last group of songs, near the end they heard feet bumping, as if someone were dancing in moccasins. Chauncey had gone to the fire and burned tobacco. Albert had asked Lynn what it might mean, and Lynn had replied, "Wait a few days, something may happen." As it turned out, Perry Jones, who had been very low, had died in the night. I was left to infer that the sign and Perry's death were connected. "The medicine had foretold."

Lynn had confirmation. While returning along the westbound tracks from hunting, he had sat down to rest on the rail near the second bend above Coldspring. "It was almost dark, but I could see a hundred yards. I heard something coming. It sounded like someone walking on the ends of the ties. I looked, but I couldn't see anyone. It stopped as suddenly as it commenced. I knew that was a sign." To Lynn, the implication was obvious. This was about the time that Perry went the long trail. As a track worker, it was natural for Perry to follow the westbound track to pick up the long trail to the hereafter.

◆5◆

I:ʔdo:s, the Celebration of the Cure

Just how the Little Water medicine and its renewal rite were related to the celebration rite called *i:ʔdo:s* bothered me from my first fieldwork. My Seneca collaborators tried to satisfy my questions, and Jesse Cornplanter (fig. 7) even gave me a sort of tutorial. When I worked with Jesse at Tonawanda during the 1930s, his constant complaint that the sequence of song cycles was different at Cattaraugus, his birthplace, and his obvious discomfort while performing with Tonawanda singers during sessions to renew the medicine, prompted me to suggest that he and I revisit the Newtown Longhouse neighborhood where he grew up and seek out the ritual holders to obtain their version.

He had prepared me with an outline of the Little Water Medicine Society and its component rituals. It is referred to as *gano:daʔ* or *niga:negaʔa:h dwaso:t,* "a little water, our grandparent." These are the generic terms for the medicine, including its rituals. The medicine society is *honontcinohgenʔ,* composed of the medicine holders, or charm holders. Jesse enumerated the following rituals:

1. Meetings to renew the strength of the medicine and straighten up the bundles. There were then three such meet-

FIGURE 7. Jesse J. Cornplanter dressed for *i:ʔdo:s,* Tonawanda, June 24, 1941. (WNF neg. 932.)

ings during the year, but anciently there were four. These regular meetings are termed *hadinoda:ya:s* or *hadinoda:yai* (the meaning of which is obscure); *hadiyenʔgwaʔye:ni,* "they have spread tobacco"; and *etciyenʔgwaʔye:ni swatcinohgenh,* "your whole society has spread tobacco for us charm holders."

2. The curing rite for administering the medicine, called *ʔeo waneganon ʔeondiyaʔdaniyenʔ,* "they will give him the water; they will strengthen the medicine." Using the medicine and then singing for it increases its power.

3. The ceremony to release the medicine after a cure: *howondiyahswaye:ni,* "they are as crows on a dead horse," or carrion. This is another term for *ʔeondiʔdonh,* the ceremony that a patient puts on following his seclusion. The first three songs are the same as the three songs of *hadihadi:yaʔs,* "going through the forest."

In May 1935, Jesse Cornplanter (Snipe clan) and I called on James Crow (Deer clan) and Jake Jack (Heron clan), then officers of the Little Water Society at Newtown. Jesse interpreted.

Six ritual holders guided the affairs of the Little Water Society at Newtown. In the first moiety were treasurer Jim Crow (Deer), Jake Jack (Heron), and Willie Green (Hawk), while Charles Sundown (Turtle), Kelly Lay (Turtle), and Albert Jones (Wolf) complemented them in the other moiety. These six were the so-called giant crows, or ravens (*gahgaʔgo:wa:*). All of the ritual holders held bundles of the Little Water medicine, which people addressed as *ongwayaʔdagehasheʔ,* "that which helps us," or "our helping grandfather" (*ongwaso:tdasheʔ*).

Moiety patterning runs strong at Cattaraugus. Not only are the six ritual holders apportioned equally between the two moieties, but they appoint two younger men, one from each side, to act as runners and officiate during the meetings as servants (*ongwahaʔsheʔ*) and door-keepers. Their office expires with each session, but the same ones are chosen to serve again at following meetings. During the 1930s, Reuben Isaac (Deer) and Henry Stevens (Wolf) were acting.

I:ʔdo:s, however, is the "play organization" of the Little Water company. Two "head ones," called "messengers" (*hadjaswas*)—likewise one from each phratry of clans, or moiety—perform as such. These were Jim Crow (Deer) and Charlie Sundown (Turtle), who were also among the six ritual holders. It was to these men that anyone about to sponsor a ritual celebration turned. One should go to the messenger for the opposite moiety to summon the medicine society members and conduct the ceremony.

I:ʔdo:s impinges on the Little Water Society in several ways. After one has taken the older medicine, composed of powdered meat from all of the meat eaters (*neh waga:yonʔ*), one is confined for four days; but after taking the newer plant medicine (*neh wase:ʔ*), one undergoes but three days of confinement. After either medicine is administered, one has to go to one of the two servants, whose duty it is to announce the ceremony for releasing the medicine.

The medicine man who administers the medicine should be of the opposite moiety to the patient. He alone may see the patient during confinement. He notifies the two servants that the patient is recovering.

When the medicine is administered, a certain group of songs says, "Etciyen?gwa?ye:ni swatcinonhgen? [they have put down tobacco for your medicine society]," which comprises the animal tutelaries and the human members as well.

The two runners, who go about the houses notifying the members, say, "Etciyaswaye:ni swatcinonhgen? [they have spread a feast for your medicine society]."

Members of the society come to the scene of the cure and confinement to help sing the release songs (*ensawenon?tga:?*). The patient is now on the way to recovery. After a patient is once revived by the Little Water medicine, and after he has properly released the medicine, he becomes automatically a member of the medicine company (*honontcinohgen?*) and of *i:?do:s,* the ritual society that will frequently celebrate his cure. Arthur Parker (1909) named this group the "Society of Mystic Animals."

I:?do:s Song Cycle

Six years after our visit to Newtown on the Cattaraugus Reservation, Jesse Cornplanter was prepared to define his father's version of the *i:?do:s* song cycle. Edward Cornplanter (Wolf clan) had written the songs down in the ledger of an old lacrosse club, from which Jesse had copied them. I made the present version as Jesse dictated and interpreted it during one night at Tonawanda (June 24, 1941). Jesse claimed that this version was that of the first people at Cattaraugus, those of the old settlement that antedated the settlement along Buffalo Creek in the late eighteenth century. The former settlement was referred to as *ganongishega:yon ga?degensgeon,* "the ancient settlement on the fetid-smelling banks." This version was formerly sung by John Jacket of the old Cattaraugus settlement, who was also the source of the 1849 text of the renewal songs (Jacket 1849).

Following some difficulty in trying to learn the songs of *i:?do:s* from John "Curly Head" Jimerson (who was later my informant at

Allegany), Edward Cornplanter, on the advice of his kinsmen, learned John Jacket's version of the songs from other old people who were no longer active singers. From the same sources, Edward learned the origin legend of the Good Hunter and a second part relating the search for the plant medicine (Parker 1908:150–56), the latter of which is recounted in the four periods of the renewal ceremony. The curing songs and the dance of the mystic animals, however, are celebrated in *i:ʔdo:s*. This clears up the mystery of the relationship between the two major ceremonies, which was never clear in later sources. The relationship may be stated as the equivalence of two pairs, each consisting of a myth and a ritual: the Good Hunter legend is to *i:ʔdo:s* as the search for the plant medicine is to the renewal ceremony (*hadiyenʔgwaʔye:ni*).

Edward Cornplanter's version of the Good Hunter legend conforms to other versions that I collected. If anything, it is more elaborate and detailed. An acorn shell held a sufficient quantity of medicine to heal the hunter, stressing the power of smallness. Bear lends body heat to counteract hypothermia. Buzzard as *gahgaʔgo:wa:* regurgitates to moisten the scalp retrieved by Pigeon Hawk. Dew Eagle dips a feather in the pool of dew on its back to provide a little water to refreshen the dried scalp. Belief in the healing power of song and dance sustains Iroquois medical philosophy. The patient memorizes the songs and learns the dance, and he contracts to form a society named *hadi:ʔdo:s* to celebrate cures. The obligation to renew ceremonies motivates continuity of tradition (Shimony 1961a).

Edward Cornplanter's version of the origin legend is unique, however, in having a second part that relates how the song (*gano:daʔ*) guided two young men in a search for the plant medicine. Narration of the journey and of obstacles encountered and overcome—windfall, morass, ravine, cataract, rapids, steep mountain—makes up the contents of Period I of the renewal ceremony. A winged light (the whippoorwill) leads to the source of the song: a giant cornstalk growing on a flat rock, its roots extending in the cardinal directions. One man chops the root to extract the medicine, and blood flows from the cut. One learns the song, which is *gano:daʔ*, returns home, and forms the medicine company. Its two branches are *i:ʔdo:s* and *niga:negaʔa:h.*

As Jesse Cornplanter interpreted the old Cattaraugus version of *i:ʔdo:s,* it began with an introduction of five to ten songs called "marching through the forests" (*hadihadi:yaʔs*). These heralded the four-part ceremony.

Part I. A prelude comprising the seventeen songs called *otadong-wahgwa:t,* "to kindle or raise up a flame." The sponsor of the ceremony or a designated singer performs this rite. These are the so-called messenger's songs at Allegany. At Tonawanda these songs are used to release the Little Water medicine following a cure. This is properly *i:ʔdo:s.*

Part II. Period of "individual songs," the so-called throwing songs. Members have their own songs used for throwing (*hodienonye:ndonʔ goenodyethaʔ*). Each member is supposed to own a particular song that was given to him, together with a rattle, when he joined the society. Some members possess sequences of three to five songs, but two songs are the norm. Persons lacking songs, having perhaps been cured by the Little Water medicine, may use any of the songs that the leader "dumps out of his bag of songs" (*wayenʔento gaenonʔ,* "he has spilled the songs"), much as he dumps the bag of rattles in the middle of the lodge.

Part III. Intermezzo, or "song in between" (*gaenonʔwetahonʔ*)— three songs, during which the leaders carry the sponsor around. The singer and his helper guide the sponsor back and forth the length of the lodge beside the fire.

Part IV. "Medicine dance song" (*ganonyahgwenʔ gaenonʔ*), or "high songs" (*heʔtgen nigaennonʔe*), literally, "high up the songs." This part was formerly celebrated in a secret medicine lodge, secured by doorkeepers, and allusions in some of the songs mention something like a sweat house. According to Jesse Cornplanter, the career of a shaman can be traced in the sequence of songs. He brags of his powers; a man wearing a blind mask enters and juggles "marbles" (stones heated to white heat); a doll is made to stand on an inverted corn mortar; the man in the blind mask knocks it over and it falls; and then it flies up in another song (*deyodonhonʔ*). The latter rite is sometimes called *ganonyahgwenʔgo:wa,* "the Great Medicine Dance," for emphasis.

Jesse elaborated on the terminology for this sequence of rites. At Newtown (Cattaraugus), *gayonweonwonʔgo:wa gahadiyaʔgon*—"the Great Sharp Point feast going through the forest" or "through the forest to the Great Sharp Point feast"—was the accepted and preferred term for the complete ceremony, which was usually held in the longhouse. The name of the ceremony with all of its parts was *gayoweonwonʔgo:wa,* "the Great Sharp Point," from *oyonwen:ʔ,* "sharp point"; but it does not always include the rite of traversing the forest, *gahadiyaʔgon* or *hadihadi:yaʔs,* "they are traversing . . ."

At Tonawanda and Allegany, however, the ceremony is named after the feature of taking in the kernels of corn that the organizer hands to invited singers, who return them to the conductor in exchange for a piece of meat that is distributed after the singing. This feature is called *ganenyonʔdonʔ,* "accepting the corn kernel."

At Six Nations in Canada, people refer to the singing of the "Great Sharp Point" as *gaiʔdoʔongo:wa,* or *gahıdohongo:wa.* The terms *gaiʔdonʔ* and *gahiʔdowonʔ* refer to the same thing, namely, *i:ʔdo:s,* although their meaning is now lost. The terms become *hadi:ʔdo:sheʔ* when society members are about to perform the ceremony, which in the vernacular is called "pumpkin shake," or simply *hadi:ʔdo:s.*

The Song Cycle

The Cornplanter version lacks the preliminary songs for marching through the forest, but Arthur Parker transcribed them at Newtown on the Cattaraugus Reservation in May 1906, in both Seneca and English. In 1941, I obtained a copy of Parker's manuscript, which is in the Parker Papers at the Rochester Museum of Arts and Sciences in Rochester, New York. Here I summarize the songs of the *i:ʔdo:s* ceremony from Parker's transcript. In English, the marching songs are as follows (Parker did not include the Seneca texts):

1. The Raven is heard by the song. (Repeated as long as the leader desires.) (The Raven's song is heard.)
2. The Raven has come. (Repeat)
3. The Raven has opened the door. (Repeat)
4. The Raven has entered. (Repeat)
5. The Raven is about to seat himself: now he is seated. (Repeat)

PART I

After the singers come in, there is an announcement, which introduces a special term, *waodiyendayei: honontcinonhgen?*, literally, "They have gathered from afar (from all the rough places) in the field, the medicine society," or, as we would say, "The medicine society has gathered from a remote field." "The marchers are the ravens, who alight in a cultivated field"—Jesse Cornplanter (JC).

The song leader raises, or kindles, the blaze, *otadongwahgwa:t*—from *odongwa*, "flame," and *o?tahgwa:t*, "he raises." ("We fan the flame," meaning we rouse ourselves—ACP ms., p. 3.)

Song raiser: "Hau? dejistawen?se:k [ho, pick up your rattles!]." In this medicine society the leading singer, who is called *daennonhgwa?tha?*, "he raises up the songs," instead of the usual *hadenottha?*, "singer," virtually conducts the ceremony. The speaker identifies him. Then it is up to him. When he is ready to begin, he tells his followers to pick up their rattles. He starts to shake his rattle and cries *gwa:?*, and his followers reply *he:.*—JC

Whenever the song raiser lays down his rattle, the others do likewise. Whenever he gets ready to resume after an intermission, he looks around and picks up his rattle.

At the end of the ceremony (Part IV), the song raiser and supporting singers each put down their rattles in a ring facing an inner circle and sit. Then the conductor picks up all the rattles, returns personal rattles to their owners, or puts them in a bag, which holds the stock or property of the society.—JC

Following are the songs of Part I (or Group I), *ota?dongwahgwa:t*, "raising the flame" or "to kindle the blaze."

Song raiser: *Hau? dejistawen?se:k*, "Ho, pick up your rattles."

1. *Oʔwasawen ne heʔe heʔe* (repeat three times)
   "It begins here."
   Waʔaheya. Response: *Heyen?* (end).

2. *Wa:ʔowasawaʔdyeʔ heʔe heʔe* (repeat three times)
   "It progresses from one (song) to another."

3. *Dayoʔwasawa:dyeʔ heʔe heʔe* (repeat three times)
   "It started from the beginning and is coming toward us (progressing)."[1]

4. *Son:sonk ne heʔe* (repeat five times—ACP)
   "Someone (or something)."

5. *Son:sonʔonkne: waʔahayonneʔe* (repeat three times)
   "Whoever it is, he is about to arrive."

6. *Dadakne heʔe* (repeat five times—ACP).
   (*Dadakheʔ,* "he is running this way," becomes *dadakne* in song.—JC)

7. *Dadakne heʔe waʔahayonneʔ* (repeat three times)
   "He is running this way" ("He has arrived"—ACP).

8. *Yohowenʔ henʔen* (three times, then repeated, for six times in all)
   "Female brant."
   (*Yehoʔowenʔ yeʔehowenʔ henen* (variants); *yehowenh,* feminine of *enowenʔ,* "brant.")[2]

---

1. Jesse argued with his father that this song should be number one, but Edward would never agree, for he had been told never to change the order.

2. This bird inhabits lake country. Its name derives from its call as heard when it is flying far off, *en:ʔ en:ʔ o: wenʔ.* It somewhat resembles the Canada goose (JC). Herbert Deignan, then curator of birds at the U.S. National Museum of Natural History, identified it as the eastern brant (*Branta bernicla*), as did ACP.

9. *Hahowen: hen?en* (repeat)
   Haho?owen: wa?ahayonne?e
   "The male brant is about to arrive, as in a floating canoe."

10. *Yehonyo ho?o yehon?onyo* (repeat six times)
    (*Yeon:yo?*, "she floats in a canoe.")
    Ye?e . . .
    Wa?aheya. Response: *Heyen.*

11. *Hahanyo ho?o hahan? anyo wa?ahanyon?*
    Hahanyo ho?o hahan? anyo wa? wa?aheya
    Response: *Heyen*
    (*Haonyo?*, "he is in a boat floating; he is about to arrive—JC; "he has come by a floating canoe"—ACP; male and female brant on the water—CJJ.)

12. *Gahgane he?e gahga?ane* (repeat three times; six in all)
    (*Gah?ga?*, Raven or Crow.)
    Wa?aheya. Response: *Heye.*

13. *Gahgane he?e gahga?ane*
    (a) *wa?ahayonne*[3]
    (a) (b) *wa?aheya.* Response: *Hyenh.*
    "Raven, Raven, Raven has come."—ACP

14. *Yeda?akhea da?a? ayeyon?on?on?* (repeat twice)
    (*Yedakhe?a daye:yon*, "she is running; she came in"; "she entered running."—ACP)
    Yowi? i? i (three times). *Hai? yenh* (end).
    (*Hai? yenh* is the ending from *ganonyahgwenh?*, the medicine dance, stating the dance tempo.)

---

3. The notations (a), (b), (c), and so forth in the songs refer to parts of the song line that are repeated in the following line. It is a kind of shorthand that is useful in the field. The texts come thick and fast, and this saves writing down all the words. In this line, for example, the word *gahgane* is repeated before *wa?ahayonne*. In the next line, both *gahgane* and *he?e* precede *wa?aheya*. Frequently, words are inverted in the second line: (a) (b) becomes (b) (a).

Here the tempo increases, beginning on the repeat following the singer's prelude. The melody also changes. The singer shakes his rattle faster to alert the chorus.

Tempo usually changes with a certain phrase—faster to dance, slower to end. Slow song tempo is called *oenonsha:ye,* from *oʔsha:yen,* "it is slow." Faster song tempo is called *oenonssno:weʔ,* from *oʔsno:weʔ,* " it is faster." Similarly, dance tempos are distinguished as "slow stick" (*oʔhnyasnhayenʔ*) and "fast stick" (*oʔhnyasno:wa*). It is as if one used a stick (*gaʔhnyaʔ*) for beating time, which is the case for some dances such as False Faces.

15. *Agaʔadenʔ ennonʔ ge e donʔhonʔ onʔ on*
     Yeʔdakheʔa dayeyonʔ onʔ on
     Yowiʔiʔi (three times), *iʔiʔiʔi* (third time).
     Haiʔ yenh (end).
     (*agadennonʔgeahdonʔ,* "I have waited for her; she was running as she entered."—ACP)

16. *Hothayoni hadakheʔeʔe* (repeat)
     Degatsinonsshendadyeʔe:
     Yowiʔiʔi (three times), *ʔi:* (repeat: abc ddd).
     Haiʔ yenh (end).
     (*Hothayoni hedakheʔ degatcinonshendadyeʔ,* "male wolf runs the length of a wide valley" [like the Genesee]).

17. (Last song)
     Dyothayoni yeʔedakheʔeʔe
     Waʔaagonhonhondyeʔeʔe
     Yowiʔiʔi (three times). *Haiʔ yenh*
     "Yon she-wolf runs atop the ridge."
     (*Waʔogonwondyeʔ, ogonwonda:dyeʔ,* "along the whole length of the ridge.")

Singer lays down rattle and others follow.

Intermission: Smoking.

Speech: The leader rises and says, "Let each member sing his own song." ("Let no one interrupt the flowing of the waters."—ACP)

PART II: INDIVIDUAL SONGS

These songs are thought to be the property of certain individual members of the society. They may be transferred between generations, as in the case of Jesse Cornplanter: "George Pierce gave me his songs, which I use." A new member of the society receives a rattle and an individual set of songs when he joins the society. These songs are called *hodiyenonyen:ndon goenondyetha?*, "they have their personal songs for throwing."

The first time through, going around the fire, members sing individual songs of a relatively serious nature, which are intended to help the sponsor of the feast, or the patient. Midway come the three mid-songs (Part III). Then comes a second period of "throwing individual songs," which is "the great hot ceremony" (*oniyonskwadaiyen?go:wa*), or sweat lodge. Indeed, the man who sponsors the ceremony is called *honiyonsko:t,* literally, "he made the sweat lodge," or ceremony. The term for sweat lodge is *wenniyonsko:t,* although none existed during the lifetime of Jesse Cornplanter (1890–1957). His contemporaries wrapped themselves in blankets and steamed themselves over a kettle of medicine. In the great sweat lodge ceremony, individuals offer a series of songs that become progressively "hot," until participants get up and dance.

Following are some examples of the individual songs that are sung in Part II at Newtown on the Cattaraugus Reservation.

1. Jesse's song (from George Pierce; see ACP ms., part 2, p. 6):
   a. *Hennewa: hene:wa:ha?* (repeat), "right now, right now."
      Ayagonon?skwade:k yagongwe? ehe, "it will burn the bed of that woman."
      Ayongenon?geye:niyak, "should she keep mocking me."
      (*Nen newa?,* "right now"; *enyagonon?skwade:k,* "her bedstead would burn" [*ganon?skwa?,* her bed; *ganonkda?,* bed; *enyo:dek,* it will burn]; *yagongwe,* "that woman"; *ayonknon?genia:k,* "should she continually imitate me.")
   b. Same song with this threat: *enyagononhsade:k,* "her house would burn."
      (These two songs imply a punishment for whoever would

dare to mock or imitate the shaman. The song has such power.—JC)

2. An example of another individual song:
   a. I think it is *gahiʔdohonʔ gayashonʔ; i:ʔdo:s* is its name.
   b. I think there is a lot of tobacco there.
   c. I think that there is a big kettle resting there.
      (These are items that the sponsor must provide at the feast named *gaiʔdo onʔ* or *i:ʔdo:s.* Singers smoke during intermissions, and they expect a full kettle to be divided among them after the ceremony is finished.)

3. A further example, recorded by Joe Logan in Canada but known at Tonawanda:
   The owl is a witch
   Surely that owl has power.

4. Hot songs (in sweat house). Example, fast tempo. (James Crow of Newtown used to sing this, and Henan Scrogg sang it at Tonawanda in the 1940s.)
   a. *Howiyahe* (repeat) *heʔ e he*
      Wahadiyonʔ nononhtcinonh
      Genʔen
      Howiya heʔe he (repeat)
      "They have all arrived of the medicine society."
      (In song, the third person plural *hon-* becomes *non-*.)
   b. Same as 4a, but second line is:
      Waʔennonjenʔ nononhtcinonh
      (*Wainonjenʔ,* "they have sat down, the medicine society.")
   c. Same as 4a, but second line is:
      Dehonnonʔtgwen hononhtcinohgenʔ
      (*Dehononʔtgwenʔ,* derived from the spoken form *deo:nonʔtwenʔ,* "they are all dancing, the medicine society.")
      Here the members jump up and dance.
   d. Same as 4a, but second line is:
      Deshodi:den . . .
      (*Deshodi:denʔ,* "they have taken flight, flushed.")

Arthur Parker, too, wrote down some individual songs from Newtown, in May 1906 (ACP ms., pp. 6–24). The Seneca texts are missing.

1. a. All the songs I know (repeat three times; then by the company).
    b. All the wild animals I know. (repeat)
    c. I know all the waters that flow. (repeat)

2. a. I built a fire and it burned.
       Then I arose
       The fire burned
       So now I am about.
       Heniwa:onh, "she would be burned, should she do likewise."
    b. *Heniwa:oh,* "her house would be burned, should she do as I did." (Compare Jesse Cornplanter's version, which lacks the preface.)

3. a. Among the flowers I am walking.
    b. Among the flowers she is walking.
    c. In the sand I am walking.
    d. In the sand she is walking.
    e. In the level forest I am walking.
       (These songs refer to the powers of, habitats of, or adventures with the medicine animals, the tutelaries, who sing in rotation.—WNF)

4. a. *Henio* (repeat four times)
       I put my song beside the Great Sharp Point.
       Gai i: hedongo:wa (gahidohongo:wa)
    b. *Hedongo:wa*
       You have overlooked my song.

5. a. I think of the name *gai i: do?* (or *-don?*) (*gahi?dowon?*).)
    b. I think there will be a great feast coming.
    c. I think there is a great kettle.

6. a. *Yo no oh he* (repeat) (?)
    b. A (female) raven.
    c. A handsome (male) raven.

7. The owl lives among the hemlocks. (Cf. Johnny John version.)

8. a. The Raven sees the feast,
       The Raven sees me about to eat.
    b. The ravens are coming up the creek.

9. a. Wolf is running through the valley. (This was Joe Logan's song.)
    b. Wolf is running where the trail lies.

10. a. *Hai i yo:* (repeat six times)
    b. He is returning. (repeat)

11. a. The good Raven (repeat three times).
    b. The good female Raven (repeat three times).
       (Songs tend to run in pairs, male and female.—WNF)

12. An example of a "hot" song; cf. Jesse Cornplanter:
    a. *Ho i ya he* (repeat three times)
    b. *Ho i ya he* (repeat three times), they (the society) have seated
       themselves.
    c. *Ho i ya he* (repeat three times), they . . . have flown away.

13. a. *Ho i ya he* (repeat three times), it has gone.
    b. *Ho i ya he* (repeat three times), the wolves are coming.
    c. *Ho i ya he* (repeat three times), the wolf pups are coming.

14. a. I have gone through the feast (repeat) (fulfilled the ceremony).
    b. I have gone through the village. (repeat)
    c. I have been through the swampland (repeat) (Reminiscent of
       Little Water renewal song, Period I).

15. a. *Wiyaheh* (repeat three times), I came from below the rapids.
       Yo ho: (repeat), I am dancing.

(Here the poetic narrative identifies the homesite of one of
the animal familiars or mentions an adventure en route to the
meeting.—WNF)

16. a. *Yo: o: o:!* (repeat), they have come, the Ravens.
    Hai eh-hi, the Ravens.
    (Crow, or properly Raven, is the familiar of the shaman singer.
    The medicine society behave as if they are ravens. Their leader,
    the song raiser, is *gahga?go:wa:,* the big Raven. Therefore his
    song speaks of their arrival, stay, and departure.—WNF)
    b. *Yo: o: o:!* (repeat), they are seated, the Ravens (the society).
    Hai eh-hi, the Ravens.
    c. *Yo: o: o:!* (repeat), they have flown away, the Ravens.
    Hai eh-hi, the Ravens.

17. (21 in ACP ms., p. 15):
    a. All of my children are beneath my wings. (repeat)
    b. All (of them), I am grandmother (to them). (repeat)
    c. I cherish my grandchildren. (repeat)
    (Medicines of all sorts occupy the status of grandparent to
    the people. The same relationship obtains between the people
    and the Little Water medicine, the False Faces, and medicinal
    herbs. Here the Raven takes the people under protective cus-
    tody.—WNF)

18. (22 in ACP ms., p. 15; cf. song 16; also song 1 of Joseph Logan's
    version):
    a. *Yo haha e hi* (repeat five times)
    b. They have come, the Ravens. (repeat)
    c. They have sat down, the Ravens. (repeat)
    d. They have flown, the Ravens. (repeat)

19. (23 in ACP ms., p. 16):
    a. *Do ni gwen: doh* (repeat twice) has peeped in the door (repeat
    twice).
    Do ni gwen doh (repeat twice), you are invited, he said, *do ni
    gwen doh.*

(*Donigwendoh,* a bird, notifies the animals of the meeting place. Its human representative goes from house to house notifying members of the society where and when to meet.—WNF)

b. *Do ni gwen doh* (repeat), tells where the ceremony will be.
Do ni gwen doh (repeat), he says it will be in the song house.
Do ni gwen doh (repeat), he is fleeing.
His tail is just visible.

20. (24 in ACP ms., p. 24):
   a. Now it shall continue to the finish, my song.
   Hai i ih (repeat)
   b. Now it is in progress, my song.
   Hai e ih (repeat)
   c. Now it has returned, my song.
   Hai e ih! (repeat)

21. (25 in ACP ms., p. 18):
   a. I did not think he was a member, the owl is his name.
   b. I did not previously think that the owl was *otgont* (malefic).

22. (26 in ACP ms., p. 18.):
   a. Now, now, I lay down the songs, now, now.
   b. Now, now, I straighten my legs, now, now. (repeat)
   c. Now, now, I stretch my body, now, now. (repeat)
   (Whole company rises and dances.)
   d. Now, now, they sway their bodies, now, now. (repeat)
   e. Now, now, they move their faces, now, now. (repeat)

23. (27 in ACP ms., p. 20):
   a. *Ho ni ga yen?* (repeat four times)
   I have expelled the disease from the woman's body, *honigayen?.*
   b. *Honigayen* (repeat four times)
   I have expelled disease from the woman's legs, *honigayen?.*

24. (28 in ACP ms., p. 21):

    a. The medicine worked;
       The song I sing is my own song.
       Hai i i: he: (repeat)
       (Cf. the recording of Joe Logan, "I think my song would help
       her, that is, if I sing it.")
    b. It will help her, my song;
       The song that I sing.
       Hai i i: he: (repeat)
    c. It will arouse (stir her body?), my song,
       The song that I sing,
       Hai i i he: (repeat)

25. (29 in ACP ms., p. 22): *Do hi ya? ya? hah; ho doh hi hi ya?* (repeat)

26. (30 in ACP ms.): *Ya ha ha hi* (repeat) *ho doh hi ya hi*

27. (31 in ACP ms.):
    a. The Wrens (repeat four times) (*djon djo?*).
    b. They are talking together. (repeat)
    c. They are thinking together. (repeat) (Cf. opening songs by
       Joe Logan.)

28. (32 in ACP ms.):
    a. *Do hi yah, do hi yah,* we made an error in our song.
    b. *Do hi yah, do hi yah,* we now correct (straighten) our song.
    c. (*Do hi yah, do hi yah,* we now will sing more carefully.

29. (33 in ACP ms.): Nonsense vocables—omitted.

30. (34 in ACP ms.):
    a. A cold spring, it is, *hai ie:h.* (repeat)
    b. We come to it, *hai ie:h.* (repeat)
    c. We seat ourselves, *hai ie:h.* (repeat)
    d. Then we sing, *hai ie:h.* (repeat)
       (A little spring where animals are wont to go and drink is
       specified in the origin legend of the plant medicine and in the
       songs of Period I of the renewal ceremony.—WNF)

PART III: MIDSONGS (CORNPLANTER)

These are the three songs known as *gaenonʔwe:tahonʔ enonwonwishonʔ*, "songs midway (in between) when they lead him around" (Parker's manuscript, part 2, p. 3, gives *onwadi awishonʔoh*, "the head singers lead . . ."). They are the treatment songs used when the medicine society cures the sponsor. If he or she is sick, members carry him or her by each arm, back and forth beside the fire, traversing the length of the house. The two leaders march the patient up and down. Part III begins with an introduction in which the lead singer calls *haiʔ* and the company responds *yenh* (an antiphonal repeated twice). The midsongs are then the following:

1. *Hodegiya hodehegiyaʔa yaʔa heʔ eehe* (repeat)
   Hodegiyaʔ heʔe hodegiyaʔ a he (repeat)
   Singer: *Haiʔ.*
   Company: *Yenh* (end).
   (*Hodegi*, "his fire is burning"; *yaʔhe:*, "the fire that he kindled is blazing.")

2. *Hoʔdeganonhsiʔden hodegi:yaʔ a heʔenhe:* (repeat)
   "Midway of the longhouse his fire burns."
   Yaʔ he::, his blazing fire.
   (In speaking, *hodeganonhsiʔden*, a rhyme word, becomes *haʔdeganohsayenʔshon*, "midway of the house.")

3. *Yehenegi:ʔ i haenenʔengiihiʔ* (repeat three times)
   Yohenenne:
   Hoʔogaʔanonʔonsayenʔ endadyeʔ ee
   Haiʔ ennengiʔ hi yohenennee
   (*Hoʔganonhsayenda:dyeʔ*, "as the house itself extends, the entire length of the house." So they do indeed walk the entire length of it—JC. "The blaze extends as far as the house"—ACP. "The firelight shines the length of the house"—WNF.)

The songs are followed (and Part III ends) with a break during which participants rest and smoke.

The last song pertains more properly to the shaman's songs of *ganonyahgwen?*, which follow. Parker says these songs are sung by the leaders of *i:?do:s* and are repeated by the company as the shaman performs his magic. Each song refers to some action of the shaman. Parker says that the people regarded the leader of *i:?do:s* and his band as "witches" and conjurors (ACP ms., part 2, p. 2).

According to Jesse Cornplanter, Newtown song leaders go through each song five times. First, the leader, standing; second, with the group; third, they march; fourth, at the far end of the house they turn and sing it again, standing; and five, they repeat the entire song marching back to their original positions.

PART IV (CORNPLANTER)

Part IV of the *i:?do:s* ceremony is the medicine dance, *ganonyahgwen?* or *ganonyahgwen?go:wa,* when all the songs for the mask worn by the shaman are included. This is Parker's "Shaman's song," or "Near the end dance" (*wadiyenon gaidot ganonyahgwen*). It consists of forty-two songs in all, beginning with three introductory songs that participants sing while seated.

1. *Gahi?dohon? wade:non? den: di i hewadenonhdendi i* (repeat)
   Gwa? he:
   (*Gai?don wadenon?hdandi,* "let *i:?do:s* commence.")

2. *Gahi?dohon? dwadennon dayon odi hedwadennon?*
   "Let us advance the medicine song."
   (In song, *hedwadennondeyo?di* in speech becomes *[he]dwadennon?hdenja:t,* "let us advance [push] it, the ceremony.")

3. *Gahi?dohon? wage:gen? ne? ho iwe? e he*
   Negahennon? ne?ho iwe?e he
   "I witnessed the ceremony in progress." ("[The song] is here walking, I saw it."—JC & WNF)
   (*Gaenon?,* "song"; *age:gen?,* "I saw," or *wage:gen* in old Seneca, "I have seen it"; *ne?ho i:we?,* "here it is walking" [the song]; *gai?don?,* "I saw it walking here.")
   (The question: Who is he [the shaman]?)

4. *Yowine: gaʔayohoʔo yohoʔo henʔenhe sodaha gawiʔine*
   Hahoʔ oho yoʔo ho (repeat)
   (*Soʔdaha gawiʔne*, "My father did not know [what] this [meant]—
   JC. Parker's song 5 [ms. p. 5]: *shodaha gawine*, "a present thrown
   [to the crowd].")

5. (Repeat lead of song 4) *sondiha hayonhonne* . . .
   "Who is the one who is going to come?"
   (The question refers to the great shaman who will arrive and
   perform all manner of magic. *Sondiha hayonhonne*, "who is he
   who will come.")

6. *Yoʔowinne? gayaha wowiʔinehe? gayaha* (repeat)
   (Meaningless, apparently, but sung to set off 4 and 5.)

7. *Waʔgensen waʔgenʔensehe:n?* (repeat)
   (Singer commences to stomp at halfway)
   Deganonda heyoʔ onon yowine yowiʔine (repeat)
   "I stomp, I stomp,
   "It echoes throughout the village, on the hills,
   "throughout the house." (three times)
   (*Oʔgensa, wagensen*, "I stomp" [bump my feet]; *deganondahayoʔ
   onon yohi: ne*, "throughout the settlement it resounds."
   Tonawanda: *ganondaʔ*, "village," but with *ononda*, "hill," "on the
   hill it resounds"—JC; or, with *deganonhska*, "throughout the
   house it echoes" [Elsina Billy-Cornplanter: *yoweson*].)

8. *Hoʔgayaʔa* (repeat) *haʔwe: hoʔdinonhsongohdon?* (repeat)
   Waʔ he:
   (Speaking: *hodinonhsongoʔhdon?*, "they went through the house."
   Jesse thought that *hodinonhsa:ni*, "they built the longhouse,"
   related to the name of the Iroquois Confederacy.)

9. (With song 10, one of two songs that speak of arrivals:)
   Yoʔ oho deyohennonga dyongwayon yoʔ oho (repeat)
   Yoʔ ohoYoʔ oho
   (*Dyohennonʔga*, "yonder song"; *dyongwayon*, "we have all come in."
   Animals [people] marching from another settlement heard the
   song afar, followed it, and have come into the lodge.—JC)

10. *Yoʔ oho deyohennonga thadiyon yoʔ oho*
"Song afar and they came in." ("There was singing when we came in.")
(*Thadiiyon,* "they [all] came in." This is sung by the other moiety, referring to the side that entered the lodge from afar.)

11. *Haiʔene: haiʔene dedwadenonh deyondihi* (repeat)
"Let us combine our songs."
(They all stand.)
(*Dedwadenondayondi,* from spoken *dedwadenonhdendi,* "our songs shall go on together"; *dedwadjeʔs,* "we combine." "We are going to put our songs together," so no song will lie idle.—JC)

12. *Do:odi do:odi dwadennonʔgehaha:t* (repeat)
"Now then, now then, let's try seriously."
(*Do:di,* "now, so then"; *dwadennongeea:t,* "let's try [endeavor] seriously [to help, to cure].")
(Halfway through the song, they start to arise, following the leader. The song itself carries the events as it proceeds. At Tonawanda, singers rise, anticipating action given in the song.—JC) (Jesse thought this silly!)

13 *O:hdenjjon honʔ onʔ onʔ* (repeat) *nagehenon hai neʔe:* (repeat)
"It is about to go; it is stirring my song; *hai neʔ e.*"
(At halfway, start dancing.)
(*ʔOhdenjon,* "it is moving, stirring, about to go"; *nagehennon,* "my own song," derived from *naage:nonʔ neʔ age:nonʔ.*)

14. Same song, but: (a ["it is moving"]) (b ["my song"]) (a) (a) (a)
"It is moving, my own song,
"It is going, it is going, it is going."

15. *Igendeʔi igendeʔhihi waʔgohononkden igendei* (repeat)
"Only I know, I know that she became ill."
End of every song: *Gwa:ʔ he:*
(*Waʔgonohonkdenʔ* becomes *waʔagononkdenʔ,* "she became ill," in speech. *Iʔgendeiʔ,* "I myself know." The medicine man is bragging

because he knows what is going to happen to her [the patient]—
JC. The singer's cry of *gwa:* at the end of every song is replaced
by *wa:* at Tonawanda.)

16. *Waʔkezenʔt* (repeat) *henhen* (repeat) *iʔdageei dodayesonʔhon* (repeat
    whole)
    "I cured her, healed her; I myself have carried the burden."
    (*Waʔkhezenʔt,* "I have cured her," from *oʔkhezenʔt; iʔdageei* plus
    dodadyesenʔ, "I have been bearing it," as if the singer came bearing
    a burden, *dakhennondaye,* which might be medicine—JC. His
    burden was the knowledge how to cure her—ACP.)

17. *Hayonwan hayonʔ onwan an haiʔih hihi haiʔihi* (repeat)
    "He of rushes . . ."
    (*Hayonwanʔ,* "he of the rushes" [or weeds]. Rushes, herbs, and
    growing plants are collectively called *oyon:waʔ*. All growing
    things—plants and animals—participate in this ceremony.—JC)

18. *Sayodenʔ sayonʔondon:ʔ haiʔihi haiʔihih* (repeat)
    "It's a blessing that she recovered."
    (*Sayo:denʔ,* "it is good, blessing"; *sayo:ndon,* "she got well, recov-
    ered." This is a blessing.—JC) (Parker has this as song 19.)

19. *Sagondenʔ sagonʔonzen:ʔt haiʔihih* (repeat)
    "I took pity on you and cured you."
    (*Saago:ndenʔ,* "I took pity on you [did you a favor]"; *sagonzenʔt,* "I
    have cured you"—JC.)

20. *Haiʔ inh jaiʔine gonyahdenʔdyedonhon* (repeat)
    (*Gonyahdendyedon,* "I took you along, made you move, walk.")
    (The sponsor or patient dances, continuing a full circuit.)

21. *Haieniyo henenʔ* (repeat four times), shorten to *haeniyo*
    (a) (b)
    "His song is good," he has good songs—*haeni:yo:.*
    (When the two were young, Joe Hemlock used to argue with
    Jesse Cornplanter favoring *haini:yo:,* "his burden is good," from

gainon?, "burden, bundle," vs. *gaeno?,* "song." Jesse felt that the *k*
phoneme replaced *g* everywhere in old Seneca. This would probably be true also of *d* and *t*.)

22. *We?endi:yo henhen wendiyo hehehen?* (repeat)
     "Good day, fine day" (because she is recovered).
     (*Wendi:yo?,* "fine day.")

23. *O?tgaenondiyondon? nongwaenon? gayo?owe*
     Haigen?ene gayo?owahi? iyo? o?o (repeat)
     "This song is pulling in opposition (off tempo),
     "Our song, to the Great Sharp Point(?)."
     (The songs are pulling in opposition as our song nears the end of
     the ceremony of the Beautiful Sharp Point.)
     (*O?tgaennondiyondo?,* "songs pulling in opposition"; *nongwaenon?,*
     "our song"; *gainiyowe:,* "how far"—JC; *haigen?enne:* [one senses
     that the ceremony is nearing the end, a Canadian expression—
     JC]; *gayonwe,* "the point" =name of ritual; *higen,* "this here," *voici;*
     gayo?onwahi:yo?, "fair, beautiful sharp point"—ACP.)
     ("This song is unbalanced, off tempo until the singer reaches the
     burden syllables in the second line. One must know the language
     to keep the song in tempo."—JC)

24. *Jihondoden jihondoden ganonhsen? ganonhshen?enhen?* (repeat)
     "Erect a tree, stand up a tree, in the center of the lodge, midway
     of the lodge."
     (*Jihondo:den?,* "erect a tree, stand up a pole" [*o?onda?*]; *gononhsen?,*
     "in the center of the house.")

25. *Yo?owihi yo?owihi gahidaniyondon? onhon* (repeat)
     "*Gai?don?* songs hang upon it (the tree)."
     (*Gahidaniyondon?* derives from spoken *gai?daniyondon?;*
     ga——niyondon?, "something hanging [ornament]"; *gahi?dowon?*
     or *gai?don?,* name of ritual. Therefore: "The *gai?don?* songs hang
     upon it [the tree].")

Regarding songs 24 and 25, Edward Cornplanter, Jesse's father,
used to say, "They have planted that tree, and in a short while it grew

to bear sparkling things that tremble, as if blown by the wind." Jesse added: "It sounds as if the *gaiʔdonʔ* songs were hanging there. Father would not agree."

The feat described in songs 24 and 25 represents one shaman's demonstration of power. Once the animal tutelaries had demonstrated such power, later people invoked animal familiars when they met to demonstrate such powers, which are such that a menstruating woman must not be in the vicinity to spoil the magic.

Jesse cited an example of failure in latter-day magic. A youngster during his day at Newtown stood his gourd rattle up on its handle in the center of the house during song 24. He held it erect by his forefinger and then tried to catch it by the handle before it fell, but it fell over anyway and smashed the gourd.

26. *Yotsigenʔengen yotsigengenhen*
     Yotsigenʔengen yotsigengenhen
     Khendaʔgehaʔ hahondenhonʔ onwiʔihi
     "Have you seen, have you seen him?
     "Bearing a branch of blueberry
     "That grows in the swamp?"
     (*Yotsigengenʔ, derived from hodjigengenʔ,* derived from *djigenʔ,* "have you seen?"; *kenhdaʔgeha,* "swamp dweller," the blueberry; *hahondenhonwi* from spoken *haondenwi,* "he is carrying a branch." Another magician enters carrying a branch or limb of the blue- berry that was planted [erected] in song 24.)

27. *Waʔkh eyo:den wakh eyo:denhen*
     Ongesaga hon:onweʔ eehe (repeat)
     "I stuck it (a dart) in her,
     "It lodged in my own mouth."
     (*Waʔkheyoʔdenʔ,* "I stuck it in her [sponsor, patient]"; *ongesagaonwe,* "it lodged in my mouth" [*gesagain*]. The shaman who sings says that he stuck a dart in her, but it lodged in his own mouth—JC. Compare "he compels her to stoop [*waʔkeiohdedenʔ*] when something is thrust in his mouth"—ACP.)

27. Three songs when a mask is used:

a. *Den? enden? den?enden?hen? wa?tgonhsayanondanon hai he he? e*
"The mask peered in."

b. *Den? enden? den?enden?hen? wadydanondahgon*
"Its whole body intruded."

c. *Yo?owihi yo?owihi watsisdaya?nondahgon*
"Embers fly about." (He tackled the embers [handled fire].)
(*Wa?tgonhsayanondahnon,* "the mask peeked in," in speaking,
derived from *dewa?tgonhso:den. Wa?dya?daya?nondahgon,* "its
whole body thrust in"; *wa?dya?do sasi,* "it exposed its body," in
speaking. *Wa?tsisdaya?nondahgon,* "it [he] embers tackled, han-
dled," derived from *wa?tsisdatganya:t,* "he has played with fire,"
in modern Seneca.)

None of the songs of number 27 refers specifically to a blind
mask, and Jesse Cornplanter never saw one. Instead, members of the
medicine society at Newtown used any black mask that qualified as a
"medicine mask." Keppler bought the Cornplanter mask, afterward
in the collection at the Museum of the American Indian, Heye
Foundation (Keppler 1941). Jesse's Tonawanda wife, Elsina Billy-
Cornplanter, volunteered that it should be a *white* mask.

28.   *Wa? ha? a wa?ha?a nehe otidaya?dendonshe?*
"Now they begin to stagger." ("Their bodies begin to sway."—
ACP)

29.   *Wa? ha? a wa?ha?a nehe otodiya?dodayeshon?*
"They commence to struggle, they tremble, their bodies quake."
(*Otadiya?dodadyeshon?on,* "their bodies contend, struggle." In chal-
lenging an opponent, one says *dendiya?doddadyeshon?,* "our two
bodies will strive for supremacy." *Detodiya?don data?,* "their bodies tremble, quake, shake.")</ />

In songs 28 and 29, the dancers act the parts given in the songs.
They stagger as if drunk, turn in opposition—pretending to wrestle,
locking arms and weaving side to side—and tremble from exertion.

30. *Yoʔ oho ganeshagon ne huiwe yo: ho:* (repeat)
    "Beneath the brush, there it is walking."
    (*Ganehsaagon,* "beneath entwining brush," in modern Seneca,
    oskawagon or *ʔoskawayenʔ,* "beneath the brush—JC after Kelly Lay.
    Ne huiwe, a transposition of *neʔ hoʔi:weʔ,* "there it is walking.")

31. *o:nenʔyai o:nenʔyai haiʔihi* (repeat four times)
    "Hot rocks."
    (Here the masker juggles heated stones, a kind of white
    quartzite or "marble," left in the fire until white hot to be tossed
    and caught.)

32. *Waʔgayaadenʔt nongwayaʔdaha:ʔ oʔjoyenʔhenʔ*
    Gwendonʔseʔ ehe waheʔe waheye he (repeat all)
    "It fell down our doll,
    "The tobacco smoke is wavering."
    (*Waʔgaya:denʔt,* or, in speaking, *dgayaʔdenʔt,* "it fell" or "falls";
    oyaʔdaʔ, "body"; *gayaʔdaʔ,* "doll"; *nongwayaʔdaʔ,* "our doll";
    oʔjoyenʔhenʔgwendo:ʔseʔ, "tobacco smoke is wavering," from
    oyenʔgwe:ʔ, "smoke," and/or *oyenʔgwaʔ,* "tobacco"; *deyawendoseʔ,*
    "it is wavering, swaying.")
    (Here the magician wearing the blind mask knocks over a doll
    that has been mysteriously made to stand on an inverted corn
    mortar. The doll was thought to have power to influence the
    smoke.—JC)

33. *Waʔgayashenʔt wagayashenhenʔt deyodeyodoʔ odenhonhonʔ*
    "It has fallen to the ground."
    (*Waʔgayaʔsenʔt,* "it has landed" in Seneca; *oʔgayashenda:t,* "it has
    settled"; *deyodenhon,* "there it has flown"; *deyo:den,* "it has flown."
    "It has landed; it lies where it has flown.")
    (First the doll drops, then it lands, and from there it starts to fly
    upward again—JC. The doll is not mentioned in versions from
    Allegany—WNF.)

34. (Here the tempo changes.)

O:nen o:nen he?tgen djonda:tha? (a) (a) (repeat)
"Now, now on high the two hold the doll."

35. (a) (a) *Hejonda:ta?* (a) (a) (repeat)
"Now, now the two have removed her (taken her away)."

36. *Jistagwenji jistagwenji deyoditaha? ha?a* (repeat)
"The two birds are conversing . . ."
(*Jistagwenji,* name of bird thought to be "tomtit" [EC]; but
Oneida *jistogeli,* near the beginning of the Logan version, is an
owl. Parker identifies them as wrens. *Deyo:dta:?,* "the two are
conversing"; *wenondo?,* "they are saying." The song is a play on the
word that the birds are saying.)

37. (The final song of the cycle:)
Ho?tgaennongondadye ho?tgaennongonddaha? djehe (repeat)
"It is the last song, the final song of the cycle."

38. Here begins a series of three songs (songs 38–40) with the same
ending. The singer identifies it, and the chorus shouts the
antiphonal *hai he he?e.* The singers and watchers know the end
has been reached. Here I give only the singer's lines:
Hai he he?e (repeat)
Deyagigonhsanegen?
"Our two faces vis-à-vis (the two singers)"
Deyagigonhsane:gen?
"Our two faces (his and mine) are together." (repeat)

39. *Hai he he?e* (repeat)
Onen sawahdandihha?ha? (repeat twice)
"Now it has departed, it has gone home."
(*O:nenh sawahdandi,* "now it has gone away";
nongwaenon?shon?hon?, "our entire songs.")

40. *Hai he he?e* (repeat)
O?wa?nonyayendonse?he? (repeat)
Gahidohon?gowa?aha? (repeat)

"Afar the medicine dance is about done,
"Yea, the great *gaiʔdonʔ* ceremony."
(From *ganon:yaʔ,* [medicine] dance, and *howaʔ/nonyayendonʔseʔ,*
"away/dance is wavering, fading." "Away from us, the medicine
dance is fading; yea, the great *i:ʔdo:s* ceremony.")
(By now the dancers are at the far end of the longhouse, going
out by the far door.)

41. *Oʔgi:ʔdahennonwenhenʔ henʔt haihe heʔe* (repeat)
    "I raise up the bundle of songs."
    Gayonweohonʔ gowahahaʔ haihe heʔe (repeat)
    "I put the songs up on the shelf of the Great Sharp Point cere-
    mony."
    (*Oʔgiʔdahennonwenhemt,* in modern Seneca, derived from *oʔgen-*
    nowenenʔt, "I raise up the song and store it overhead." This is as if
    the singer picks up the whole bundle of songs, like a bag of rat-
    tles, and stores them overhead in the loft or shelf beneath the
    rafters of the longhouse—JC.)

42. (Fast tempo:)
    Yoʔ haʔ haheʔ deganonʔgeodadyeshonʔ (repeat)
    "The two horned ones are contending."
    (*Deganonʔgeodadye:shonʔ,* "the two horned ones are contesting";
    deniyaʔdadyeadye:shonʔs, "their two bodies are opposed." "Possibly,
    the horned ones were the final charm animals to leave."—JC)
    Gwa: gwa: he:
    Gwa: gwa: he:
    (End)

The singer now speaks: "Enswehe:k o:nen owenniyonsgwanos
swatcinonhgenʔshonʔ [you all shall now think that the steam of your
medicine lodge has cooled!]" (bear in mind now that the steam has
cooled in your sweat lodge). Here the singers lay their rattles down
in a circle, the gourds at the hub and the handles radiating as spokes.
The conductor picks them up and returns them individually to their
owners.

Coldspring Variants

From my first summer at Coldspring (1933), on the Allegany Reservation, my host, Jonas Snow, endeavored to explain to me the nature and distinctions of *i:ʔdo:s* ceremonies. It soon became apparent that one might adhere to one or several orders of ceremonies, ranging from simple *i:ʔdo:s,* with singers chosen at random, to the composite, moiety-structured *hadihadi:yaʔs* ("going through the forest") ceremony with a False Face.

Later that summer, Chauncey Johnny John, who became my mentor in such matters, outlined the structure of *i:ʔdo:s.*

Membership consists of persons who were seriously ill and to whom the ritual brought relief, or who dreamed about the ceremony and its ritual props. Clairvoyants interpret dreams and prescribe specific ceremonies.

Each member has a song and a rattle. A sack of rattles resides with a song holder. Individuals learn the complete cycle of songs by listening and participating, although sessions to teach the songs occur, when one should burn tobacco and notify the animal tutelaries.

Of the two kinds of *i:ʔdo:s,* the one Chauncey belonged to was the "traversing the forest" order, including the masker, which he conducts and I describe in chapter 6. It features moiety separation, social distance, approach, and reciprocity. Three songs notify the host moiety that relief is on the way; the procession enters the lodge, sings two songs circling the fire counterclockwise, and stands before the empty bench across the fire from the hosts. As the visitors enter and circle the fire, the host moiety sings two songs together with the visiting moiety.

The conductor of the visiting moiety speaks, asking what his hosts desire: "Now we are here, we want to know what you desire, what is expected of us." In reply, a speaker from the host's moiety tells the visitors what is expected of them. He informs them who has sponsored the ceremony and assures them that he or she has everything ready: tobacco for the animal tutelaries, berries for the singers on both sides, and, at the end, meat and pig's head and hulled corn soup for everyone, and mush for the masker. There must be a piece of meat for each singer. There are eight men, four on each side, ideally a representative of each of the eight clans, besides a conductor on each side, which requires eighteen pieces of meat.

Tobacco is the main thing. All visitors must bring Indian tobacco (*Nicotiana rustica L.*) and put it in the corn-husk tray toward the invocation. They choose a man from the opposite moiety to make the invocation, which is addressed to all the animals that comprise the medicine society—the *honontcinohgen?*.

(Chauncey did not mention the "messenger's songs.")

Throwing a song. Each man of the visiting moiety in turn sings one to three songs solo, addressing the host's side across the fire. Then the visiting speaker calls upon the host's side to sing, an act called "putting it over the fire." The host's or sponsor's moiety reciprocates, singing one at a time.

Throwing songs back and forth over the fire. The sponsor's side leads off the singing. First, a man on the sponsor's side sings, and then a man on the opposite bench sings. Then the second man on the sponsor's side sings, and a second man on the opposite bench follows, and so it goes until all have sung.

The round dance. The leader is of the opposite moiety. As he sings, a man from the sponsor's moiety walks over and sings with him. The two leaders must be of opposite sides. The rest fall into line carrying rattles.

At the sixtieth song (songs 48–49 in the recording), near the end of the round dance, the masker enters, carrying a turtle rattle (*ganyahden? ha?no:wa?*). He dips his hands in the hot ashes and blows on the head and body of the sponsor, an act that will cure anything one has. He then joins the dancers at the end of the line, groaning in his inimitable way like the wild one in the woods. At the end of the dance the masker goes out, the headman awarding him tobacco as he departs.

Closing. Someone from the host's side speaks, thanking the other moiety for its efforts, for what it has done. The host who puts up the ceremony may not speak; it is a rule that the host may neither sing nor speak when he sponsors a party for the medicine company. Invitation corn is collected at this point.

Feast. Four pieces of meat (for as many singers) on each bench. A pig's head split longitudinally is passed to both sides. Recipients cry like crows, *ga? ga:?,* as they attack the meat.

The kettle (boiler) of soup is set down in the middle of the floor, and members push their pails out. A man of the opposite moiety ladles out the soup. Mush goes to the man who impersonated the masker and to all present who want any.

Informant statements about ceremonies run to ideal structure and personal experience. They take on new meaning to the ethnologist when he observes performances of specific rituals. Chauncey Johnny John conducted the performance of *hadihadi:ya?s* that I witnessed and photographed with the late Richard Congdon of Salamanca, New York (Charles Congdon's son), in the summer of 1940. The Henry Redeye household grew weary of my questions, hung the kettle for my benefit, and discharged the ceremonial obligation of a relative.

Essential *I:?do:s*

During June 1940 at Coldspring, Sherman Redeye (Snipe clan), who adhered to the least order of *i:?do:s* and frequently sang for it, helped me systematize the essentials of this order. The term *i:?do:s,* or *hadi:?do:s,* refers to boiling something, possibly the songs (*gahi:?donhon*). It is a branch of the medicine company. Members celebrate the ritual of the order that assisted in their cure; at Coldspring, there are three orders of membership and three degrees of ritual:

1. *I:?do:s,* which omits the songs referring to the entrance and participation of the masker, but includes the last four songs.
2. *I:?do:s* with *gagonhsa?,* the ceremony with the mask. This rite is called *gayoweonhwonh,* literally, "gathering the thorns," or "thrusting the sharp point in solution." It is also called

ganonyahgwenʔ, from the name of the round dance in which a masker participates (Part II of the song texts; see chapter 6.)

3. *Hadihadi:yaʔs,* or *gahadiyaʔgon,* "they are cutting through the forest," so named for the marching songs of the visiting phratry, who come over the forest path to the feast site. It is also called *gayoweohgo:wa:,* literally, "great gathering the thorns," but commonly "the Great Sharp Point." The act of the visitors returning invitation corn gives rise to a third name, *ganenyonʔdonʔ.* This is the longest ritual, and it includes the preceding two.

Curing songs. A special series of curing songs follows the first period of *i:ʔdo:s* and precedes the dance songs of *ganonyahgwenʔ.* Only certain sponsors who are sick and require the services of the society request them. They are called, appropriately, *oenuiʔah,* "song that is deranged," or "hot songs."

Time. The medicine society meets and sings the appropriate order of ritual whenever a member puts up a feast.

Place. The society meets at the longhouse or in a private dwelling. The longhouse affords the advantage of space, but some families habitually use their own homes or the house of a relative. Others prefer the longhouse.

Feast. (1) Hulled corn soup (mush in Canada); (2) meat—a pig's head is preferred; (3) mush for the mask (*gagonhsaʔ*); (4) two pails of berry juice (*oya:gi:*); (5) sacred tobacco for the invocation.

Ritual equipment. (1) Gourd, pumpkin, or squash rattles (fig. 8). Individuals bring their own; however, the society at Coldspring had two sacks of rattles, one of which Cornelius Abrams (Beaver clan) kept. Chauncey Johnny John (Turtle), who raised gourds, had the other. Frank Abrams (Wolf) and then Clarence White preceded Cornelius as keeper. There should be a sack of rattles for each phratry of four clans, but in 1939 they were obliged to borrow a sack for the opposite phratry. (2) A wooden face mask, either black or red. Color is unimportant, but I sensed a slight preference for black, which was used in the ritual that I observed. (3) A turtle rattle.

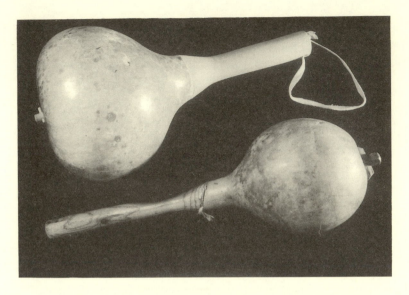

FIGURE 8. Gourd rattles of the Tonawanda Little Water Society.
Courtesy of Great Lakes Artifact Repository, Buffalo, New York.

Purpose. In response to a dream or the anniversary of a cure, whenever a member can afford it. Individuals vary in how they fulfill their obligation. One woman was thought overzealous in sponsoring all kinds of rites.

Moiety structuring. Rather than regular officers, someone is requested to take charge of the ceremony. He is called *hasdeisthaʔ*. Another man acts as messenger (*hajaswas*), to invite the members. The third principal is the sponsor or host, *godensho:nni*. She usually gets her husband or someone of her own moiety who knows how to conduct the ceremony to act in this capacity. For common *i:ʔdo:s*, anyone will do.

The conductor notifies the members. Where the phratries are involved, he invites the members of his own moiety and enlists another conductor of the opposite moiety to invite an identical number of members of his side. The latter finds the man to furnish and wear the mask. Each conductor appoints a lead singer.

The meeting. The sponsor's moiety goes directly to the longhouse to await the other side. Her moiety are as siblings (*hennondennohjonʔ*).

The opposite moiety goes to a nearby house. They are as "cousins" (*hona:ʔsishenʔ*) to the sponsor's side. (My informants, Sherman and Clara Redeye, did not think of the two phratries [moieties] as siblings and cousins.)

The opposite moiety ("the other side") departs from the neighboring house and marches, singing, toward the meeting place. Sherman thought of this as "going over the grade [path]" (*yondonyawen:sthaʔ*, derived from *yonya:deʔ*, "grade" [path], which is what they sing as they march over the grade to the meeting place.) It is unfortunate for anyone who arrives late and doesn't know the songs: he must enter the meeting singing the marching songs. Clara recalled an incident involving a man who thought he was late and reached the meeting place ahead of his brothers, who had not yet departed from the neighboring house.

The marchers sing four songs:

1. His voice sounds.
2. He approaches.
3. He enters the door.
4. They sit down in the middle of the house.

They are the ravens in procession to the meeting. As the visitors arrive inside the meeting place, the moiety of the sponsor stands and helps sing. The visitors enter, turn right, pass before the singing hosts on their right, and circle the fire, turning left (counterclockwise) to stop in front of the vacant bench (fig. 9). The meeting then consists of the following events:

1. All sit down and quit singing.
2. A speaker of the visiting moiety returns thanks to the spirit-forces from earth to sky (*ganon:yonk*).
3. The two conductors gather all the rattles, tobacco, and berry juice and assemble them with the corn soup and pig's head

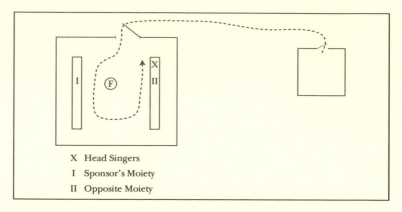

FIGURE 9. Floor plan and seating arrangement for the *hadihadi:ya?s* ceremony at Coldspring, 1940.

near the fire for the invocation. The invoker must be of the opposite moiety to the sponsor (Henry Redeye).

Intermission. The headmen pass the berry juice.

4. a. The messenger's songs (*hajaswas hoenon?*). The leader of the opposite moiety sings first, some twenty songs, which others join. These are the regular *i:?do:s* songs. (Sherman sang these for me; I took partial texts, but I did not record them.)

   b. Throwing a song. Now the headman of the visiting moiety directs his party to sing one by one. Rotation is counter-clockwise, a man singing several songs ad lib. Each man "throws a song across the fire" (*wondyiennondi?*) to the sponsor of the feast.

   c. "Putting it over the fire" (*wadizeonwen:, from gadzeot, odzeon*, "a burning fire." "They put (throw) it across the fire" to the moiety of the sponsor. Now in turn the moiety of the sponsor sings in rotation, the same way, commencing with the headman. Each man sings his own song(s).

5. Intermission. While the singers rest:

   a. A speaker announces what will follow. He announces who will sing *ganonyahgwen?*, the round dance, and who will lead it.

     b. The curing songs (*owenuiʔah*), when included, come at the end of this intermission, between two periods of throwing songs. When this part of the ritual is performed, the speaker announces it at this time.

     c. Pass berry juice.

6. Throwing songs back and forth over the fire. Now they sing again, but this time the sponsor's side leads off. Individual members of the society sing alternately back and forth across the fire from one another, first the sponsor's moiety and then the visiting moiety: "They throw songs at each other" (*wainon-dehnoʔya:k*). Thus each man sings his song until everyone has led a song.

7. The round dance:

     a. "They go right from throwing songs into the round dance. The leader is always from the moiety of the sponsor. They continue until the end of song 54" (in the texts recorded by Chauncey Johnny John).

     b. The mask. "In the middle, you will see *gagonhsaʔ* [the mask] come in at the fortieth song." (It is the fortieth song in the Frank Abrams version, which Sherman sings. Chauncey Johnny John sings a different version.) The mask stays in the dance during twenty songs. He dances around using the same dance steps, peering at watchers to discover members not participating, whom he forces to join the dance. He follows the dance, marshalling the dancers. (My informants did not know any origin legend to explain the entrance of the masked conductor.) The masker stays until a particular song (50 in the Abrams version) says, "Ashes he is scattering about," which is the signal for the masker to go to the fire and blow ashes on the head of the sponsor in the approved False Face manner. During the last song, the conductor gives the masker some tobacco, and he goes out.

        The masker among the Senecas no longer juggles hot stones. Elijah David of Tonawanda, however, when visiting

in Canada early in the century, witnessed a shaman handling hot stones. He rubbed his hands over the heated
stone and applied his hands to the patient's head (WNF
Seneca Field Notes, 1934, II: 22).

8. The speaker returns thanks again, this time to the messengers
   and conductors (the headmen), the song leaders and singers,
   and the crowd that came to watch.

9. The feast:

   a. The two conductors collect invitation corn from each
      singer in his moiety. The invited men who participated
      must pay a kernel of corn to the conductor of his side
      (moiety) before he may receive a chunk of meat, usually a
      quarter-pound of salt pork.

   b. Passing the pig's head. Properly, there should be one for
      each side (moiety), or else a single head is split longitudi-
      nally and a half goes to each side. The two conductors pass
      the halves to their respective sides.

   c. The kettle of hulled corn soup is ladled in equal portions
      to all comers on a signal to put their pails down.

   d. Mush for the masker. The masker returns unmasked and
      sits with his fellows for the distribution of the feast.
      Everyone receives some mush. The masker does not exit
      with mush, but the actor comes back for it, like anyone
      else.

10. "Fly away in all directions." As the mystic animals in human
    form requickened the Good Hunter and, assuming their ani-
    mal forms, scattered to the four winds, so the members of
    the medicine society pick up their pails and walk the roads by
    night.

◆6◆

Observations at Coldspring

My Seneca tutors had prepared me to observe actual performances of the *i:ʔdo:s* ceremony by pointing out the significant parts of the ritual that make up a pattern of sequence. But participating ritualists perform their roles as individuals, and any given performance of a ceremony takes on the character of their presence. Specific celebrations vary according to the sponsor's obligation, who the conductor and lead singer are, which version of the song cycle the conductor favors, and who shows up to listen or participate.

On September 13, 1939, I observed a *hadi:ʔdo:s* ceremony held at Coldspring Longhouse for Jesse Armstrong (Bear clan) and/or his wife (Deer clan). The layout of the room and the seating arrangement are shown in figure 10. The numbers in the diagram correspond to the following list of participants:

1. William Cooper (Snipe clan)
2. Albert Jones (Snipe)
3. Arthur Johnny John (Beaver)
4. Jesse Armstrong (Bear), host
5. Amos Johnny John (Wolf), song leader in Part I
6. Levi Baptiste (Budi:s), Cayuga clairvoyant visitor

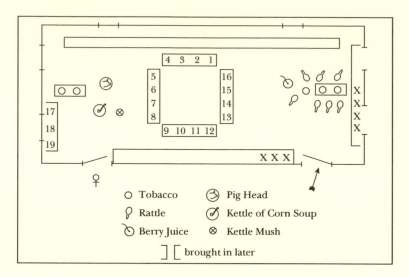

FIGURE 10. Floor plan and seating arrangement for the *hadi:ʔdo:s* ceremony at Coldspring, 1939.

7. Clarence Watt (Heron?)
8. Chauncey Johnny John (Turtle), song leader in Part IV
9. Henry Redeye (Bear)
10. Amos Redeye (Heron)
11. Hiram Watt (Deer)
12. "Chief" Cusick, Canadian visitor from Six Nations
13. Jonas Snow (Hawk)
14. Chauncey Lee (Turtle)
15. Jake Logan (Snipe)
16. Avery Jimerson (Bear)

These sixteen participants, comprising the elite of Coldspring in
addition to two visitors from Six Nations, occupied four facing
benches in a square. The occupants of the benches along the walls
were, on the women's end, number 17, Geneva Jimerson (Heron),
cook; number 18, the matron (Bear); and number 19, unknown. The
*X*s along the other two benches indicate women, boys, and Clayton

White (Wolf), who came late to listen and get some of the feast. Other than the women cooks, these were nonparticipating observers, including myself.

Order of Ceremony

A. Afternoon preliminary.
    1. Conductor notifies members and distributes kernels of corn.
    2. Cooking at the longhouse kitchen.
B. Ceremony and feast at the longhouse at night.
    3. Thanksgiving by speaker, and announcement governing the nature and content of the ceremony and who will perform what roles.
    4. Invocation with tobacco at fire.
    5. Period of smoking while conductor distributes rattles and singers put them under benches. Conductor passes berry juice. Recipients greet tutelaries.
    6. Part I, *gahi:donʔ,* led by number 5, Amos Johnny John (resembles Part II of *hadiyenʔgwaʔye:ni*).
    7. Intermission: smoking and passing berry juice.
    8. Part II, "throwing songs." First round of individual songs, clockwise in sequence of enumeration.
    9. Intermission: as above.
    10. Part III. Second round of individual songs.
    11. Intermission: finish berry juice and tobacco. Speaker announces masked dancer's entrance.
    12. Part IV, *ganonyahgwenʔ,* the dance led by numbers 8 and 2, of opposite moieties.
        a. Lead regular progression of ± forty songs.
        b. Clear away benches for round dance—side-stepping heavily at ± ten songs, until reaching ± fifteen songs.
        c. Masker: Jonas Snow (Hawk; opposite moiety to sponsor), number 13, goes out men's door and returns by women's door wearing black mask, carrying small turtle rattle. Joins dancers, making others keep in line. Leads sponsor

to fire; blows ashes on head, hands, shoulders. Rejoins
round dance, assumes lead, buffoonery with 6 and 8.
Breaks up the dance, receives tobacco from conductor,
and departs by women's door.

13. Terminal feast: replace benches; thanks to participants; finish
berry juice; announce next *hadiyen?gwa?ye:ni;* conductor
passes pig's head among singers; chunks of meat to main participants; distributions counterclockwise; call to set down
pails; conductor fills pails; masker distributes mush.

Comments

I went back to my sources at Coldspring to find out how the mask
became associated with the medicine society. John Jimerson talked
about a white mask in *i:?do:s* but could give me no information about
how the mask joined the medicine society. For as long as he could
remember, a mask had appeared in the round dance of *gayoweo?onh,*
"Sharp Point." He said, "Near the end of the songs, *gagonhsa?* comes
in and stays till the end to doctor the one who puts up the ceremony."

John had a special "white mask" that he used whenever he sponsored *hadi:?do:s.* He loaned the mask to the person appointed to
impersonate the mask so that it might doctor someone. He claimed
not to have made this mask but that it came down to him from his
father, Sam Jimerson. (This may be the white mask that Chauncey
Johnny John recalled having seen in Sam's feasts.)

If each member of the society should have a special mask for this
ceremony, practice at Coldspring denied it. Any old mask would do,
preferably black. But as for the blind mask in the New York State
Museum collection, John had never seen a blind mask in use at
Cattaraugus.

Chauncey Johnny John neither knew nor had heard of blind
masks in *i:?do:s.* Nor did he have an explanation for how or when the
mask got into the ceremony. It had simply been there as long as he

could remember. "I used to hear my father telling about the begin-nings of *niga:nega?a:h,* but he never talked about the origin of *i:?do:s.* The two are the same medicine society [*honontcinohgen?*]. But there are three varieties of *i:?do:s*":

1. *I:?do:s* (no mask), four days after taking the medicine
2. *Gayoweo?onh* (with the mask, *gagonhsa?*)
3. *Gayoweo?onhgo:wa* (a second kind with mask), "when they come marching from another house singing. They must be singing when they enter. A single person coming late must enter singing. That is why they all get there on time. When all of my men [of his moiety] reach the designated place, then I go in. We sing three songs outside, and one inside the lodge—four marching songs." This is *hadihadi:ya?s,* "cutting through the forest."

Chauncey and I talked about his role in managing such a cere-mony the afternoon before his undertaking the role as conductor for the moiety opposite that of the sponsor. Florence Crouse had been there to ask him to lead the visiting party. As a Hawk in the other moiety, she should have given all of the invitation corn to Hiram Watt (Deer), of her own moiety, and Hiram should have come to Chauncey (Turtle), of the other moiety. Hiram did enlist Sherman Redeye (Snipe), Clarence Watt (Heron), Chauncey Lee (Deer), and Albert Jones (Snipe)—all of his own moiety.

For the other side, Chauncey enlisted Henry Redeye (Bear), Amos Johnny John (Wolf) (his own son), and Richard and Arthur (Beavers) (his two grandsons).

The absence of a Hawk clan member raises the question, were the clans formerly equally represented?

There was yet no corn provided for the headman.

Chauncey planned to ask Henry Redeye or his own son Amos to make the announcements, inasmuch as he, Chauncey, would do all of the singing.

Duties of the Sponsor or Feast Maker (*Godensyo:ni*)

Florence Crouse, a first-time sponsor, consulted with members of her Hawk clan lineage—her mother (the clan matron) and her mother's sister—as to what was expected of her.

Each member of the order of *hadihadi:ya?s* has a set of kernels of corn for inviting the singers, which that member keeps from meeting to meeting. These kernels of corn acquire a potency from the ritual that is believed to infect nonmembers with their malefic power. Recipients become ill, "poisoned" in the vernacular, and they have to have the ceremony.

Things do not always go smoothly in Seneca society, as the following case illustrates.

The sponsor remarked to me, "I guess they are afraid of this ceremony. Last night, I met my sister on the bridge and asked her to take these kernels of corn and give them to her husband to summon the society. My sister did not want to accept those kernels of corn because then she might herself have to put up this kind of feast."

Later that evening, the sister and her husband called at the house of the mother, the Hawk clan matron. The husband had previously said that he would accept the role of going house to house to invite the members on his side, providing the sponsor would arrange permission to secure the neighboring house as the place where the other moiety of singers might start. (Apparently the sponsor neglected to do this.)

The sponsor continued, "That evening I gave half of the corn to my husband so that he could go around summoning members of his moiety to sing. Next morning I got him up early to go after firewood before breakfast, and he got mad and said that I had not arranged the matter of the neighboring house. Whereupon he came over here to my mother's house and returned the corn, saying that we [his wife's relatives] were always 'double-crossing him,' whatever he meant by that.

"Then as sponsor I turned to Hiram Watt (Deer clan) of my moiety. I gave half of the invitation corn to Hiram. He told me to go upriver and give the other half to Chauncey Johnny John (Turtle) for the other moiety."

The sponsor remarked on Hiram's senility. Chauncey commented on Hiram's laziness—that Hiram should have accepted all of the corn from the sponsor and himself brought half to Chauncey as conductor for the opposite moiety. The sponsor was new to the game, and Hiram let her run his errand.

The sponsor said further: "When I went up to Chauncey's and gave him the corn, telling him I wanted him to serve as conductor for *ganonyahgwen?*, he laughed at me. I should have said *gayoweongo:wa*. Then he asked me who was the other conductor . . . that [as a matter of protocol between moieties] that person should have approached him."

It is clearly a rule: the sponsor should enlist a conductor of her own moiety; he approaches a conductor of the opposite moiety and gives him half of the corn; and then they each distribute it to their respective side. Each invited person must keep the kernel of corn that he receives from the conductor and bring it to the feast. Otherwise he gets no meat. At the feast the sponsor collects all of the corn and keeps it for another, future ceremony. Evidently the present sponsor had lost hers from a previous ceremony.

Besides, each invited singer must bring a small packet of tobacco as his contribution to the invocation.

For the feast at the end of the ceremony, the sponsor must provide (1) a pig's head, which is split in halves, one for each moiety (the singers of the moiety opposite the sponsor's take their half outside the lodge for a separate feast; the other half is consumed inside the lodge by singers of the sponsor's moiety); (2) ten chunks of side pork for the singers; (3) a boiler full of hulled corn soup. (In this case the sponsor's mother provided the white corn, and the sponsor hired her mother's sister to leach it with wood ashes. This cost fifty cents.)

These three items were assembled at the sponsor's mother's house. There, her sister's husband hauled water, cut firewood, and assisted the women cooks, who boiled water and added the meat, which they left to boil slowly all day. Later they added beans.

Ritual Props

Besides the usual *i:?do:s* props—gourd rattles—no one seems to know how the mask entered the medicine society ritual. My sources knew no origin legend that might explain the mask's appearance midway through the ceremony. My hosts endeavored to explain it. "Long ago in the generation of the great-great-grandfathers, someone must have held a charm [*hotcinon?genda?*], which called for the entertainment of the False Face in the *i:?do:s* society ritual. Then his children, and their children, who became members by being included in the celebrations of their elder, continued to include the False Face in *i:?do:s* until it became an integral part of the ritual."

Although Allegany sources held that no special masks belonged to the medicine society, they usually selected a black mask as being more powerful. John Jimerson's white mask, which he restricted to his own use, was the exception (cf. Fenton 1987: 36).

The Great Sharp Point Ceremony

The foregoing discussion prepared me to observe a performance of *gayoweon?go:wa* (the Great Sharp Point) for a little girl of the Hawk clan in 1940. Afterward I read my notes back to Sherman Redeye, who commented. Here I summarize the ceremony, and in chapter 7, I offer more detail on the texts of the songs, which I recorded the following year.

Hiram Watt (Deer clan) and the singers whom he had invited to represent the sponsor arrived at the appointed house of ceremony about ten o'clock. They seated themselves on a bench to the right of the door and put their rattles under the bench.

The party of the opposite moiety, led by Chauncey Johnny John (Turtle), passed by the house and assembled at the house of Henan Crow, not far down the road.

About 10:20 P.M., marchers were heard approaching on the road and path. They sang two songs. On the third song the leader (messenger) led his party into the lodge. Chauncey paused at the door. The first singer carried a bag of rattles; the second, a pail. The floor plan is shown in figure 11, and the participants were the following:

I. Sponsor's moiety:

1. Florence Crouse (Hawk), sponsor, feast maker
2. Hiram Watt (Deer), conductor
3. Johnson Jimerson (Hawk)
4. Clarence Watt (Heron)

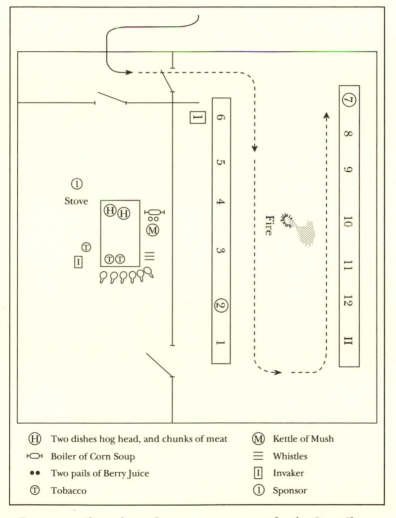

Ⓗ	Two dishes hog head, and chunks of meat	Ⓜ	Kettle of Mush
⊂⊃	Boiler of Corn Soup	≡	Whistles
••	Two pails of Berry Juice	Ⅰ	Invaker
Ⓣ	Tobacco	①	Sponsor

FIGURE 11. Floor plan and seating arrangement for the Great Sharp Point ceremony at Coldspring, 1940.

    5. Sherman Redeye (Snipe)

    6. Chauncey Lee (Deer)

II. Visiting moiety:

    7. Chauncey Johnny John (Turtle), conductor and song leader

    8. Amos Johnny John (Wolf)

    9. Wesley Dowdy (Beaver)

  10. Richard Johnny John (Gwende) (Beaver), song leader

  11. Arthur Johnny John (Beaver)

  12. Henry Redeye (Bear), invoker

Visiting moiety enters. The entering party files past with the sponsor's moiety on the right. The headman of the sponsoring moiety sits at the far end of the bench, away from the door. There, the entering leader turns left around the symbolic fire, to halt at the near end of the bench opposite the sponsor's moiety. Thus, the two leaders (conductors)— numbers 2 and 7 in figure 11—sit diagonally opposite each other.

    The sponsoring moiety, seated, sings two songs with the visitors, who remain standing until the end of the entering song (fig. 12).

FIGURE 12. The sponsor's moiety (seated) sings two songs with the visiting moiety (standing). Standing, from left: Chauncey Johnny John, Amos Johnny John, Wesley Dowdy, Richard Johnny John, Arthur Johnny John. (WNF neg. 1940.II.50.)

They then sit down. The two moieties sing a fourth song together, seated, and put their rattles under the bench.

Thanksgiving. The speaker, appointed by the conductor of the visiting moiety, returns thanks to all the spirit-forces from earth to sky—the *ganon:yonk* (fig. 13). At the end of *ganon:yonk,* before sitting, the speaker of the visiting moiety asks the sponsoring moiety, "What do you want? Who sponsored the feast? What is it for? And what is expected of us during our visit?" A speaker for the sponsoring moiety, in this case Sherman Redeye, replies (fig. 14).

Invocation. The conductors (2 and 7) collected rattles from their respective sides and together piled them near the fire (stove). Although it appeared that the conductor for the sponsoring side had

FIGURE 13. The speaker for the visiting moiety, Henry Redeye (Bear clan), returns thanks to the spirit-forces. (WNF neg. 1940.II.51, Richard B. Congdon photo.)

FIGURE 14. The speaker for the sponsor's moiety, Sherman Redeye (Snipe clan), replies. (WNF neg. 1940.II.52.)

the most responsibility, actually the conductor for the visiting opposite moiety was in charge. He collected tobacco from members of his side, as did the conductor for the sponsor's side. They put the tobacco in a saucer (anciently a twined corn-husk tray), together with tobacco provided by the sponsor.[1] The conductor for the sponsor's side made ready the fire and placed a chair for the appointed invoker (12), who seated himself with the dish of sacred tobacco and began the invocation (see Appendix A for text). The sponsor stands near the fire (fig. 15).

The invocation over, the singers pass the remaining tobacco, fill their pipes, and smoke. The conductors pass the berry juice among the singers with the usual offertory and response described in previous contexts (fig. 16):

Conductor: *O:nenh endwayen?gonwai,* "now let us wash the tobacco away!"

Sponsor or singer: *?O?tgwononyon? swatcinonhgen?shon?,* "I thank (greet) you of the medicine company."

I:?do:s, the messenger's songs (fig. 17). The conductor of the visiting opposite moiety addresses his side: "Now pick up your rattles." Presently they stand. He sings:

1. Let us try to cure her.
2. We have tried.
3. I will stomp. (repeat three times) It will resound through the fields even.
4. I did stomp. (repeat three times) It resounded through the fields.
5. It is moving. (repeat three times) We are all staggering.
6. It is going on. (repeat three times) We went staggering.
7. It is under way. (repeat three times)

---

1. When the two conductors collected and distributed, I observed that they proceeded from alternate ends of the facing benches, moving in opposite directions (from 6 toward 2 and from 12 toward 7), so that their combined movements were counterclockwise (*o?watciondase?*). Each had the bench on his right. Only in *?ohgi:we:,* the Feast of the Dead, as in the hereafter, do circuits go clockwise.

FIGURE 15. Henry Redeye performs the tobacco invocation as the sponsor stands by. (WNF neg. 1940.II.53, Richard B. Congdon photo.)

FIGURE 16. The conductor, Hiram Watt, passes berry juice. Johnson Jimerson is seated on left. (WNF neg. 1940.II.54, Richard B. Congdon photo.)

FIGURE 17. The messenger's songs (seated). (WNF neg. 1940.II.55.)

Having sung the messenger's songs, the lead singer says, "Neʔho nonʔgatgwe:ni:ʔ swatcinonhgenʔshon? [that is the best that I can do for your medicine society]." (The order and content of these prelim-inary songs differ in the 1941 recordings by the same singers, which follow in chapter 7.)

Individual songs. Men of the moiety opposite to the sponsor's begin. Conductor II—Chauncey Johnny John, the conductor for the opposite moiety—instructed his bench, saying, "Sigwa: end-wonsa:wen? [at the far end, let us commence]."

Henry Redeye (12) began by singing two or three songs ad lib (fig. 18). His son, Sherman, explained: "They have to begin at the far end of the bench away from the Conductor II, so that the individual singing proceeds counterclockwise around the fire." Singers are cautioned, "Don't bump your feet!" Both benches join in singing the repeats.

When the individual singing reaches Conductor II (number 7), he does not sing but says, "*Waʔagwahdzeowe:n* [we put it over (across) the fire]." On the sponsor's bench, singing again starts away from Conductor I, Hiram Watt (number 2); I observed that the singing

FIGURE 18. Henry Redeye, on right, opens the individual songs.
(WNF neg. 1940.II.56.)

went from 12 to 8 and then from 6 to 2. Each man sang two to four songs, and others joined in on the repeat. Singers shake rattles vibrato or twirl them circularly before coming down on the measured beat of the chorus.

Sherman Redeye, acting for Conductor I, spoke for the sponsor's moiety. He, too, said, "Sigwa: endwonsa:wen? [let us begin at the far end]." The man at the far end of the bench began to sing. The individual singing progressed down to 3, the man sitting next to the conductor. Conductor I (acting for the sponsor) does not sing.

Intermission. Now the initiative passes back across the fire to Conductor II, who is actually the headman. He says, "Endwado-inshen? da?ziu: [let us rest a little while]." The singers smoke. The berry juice is passed with the usual greeting to the society.

Deranged songs in a vacant house. Conductor II announces what is to follow: "Now we are about to commence what is called *owen-nui?ah,* 'the song is deranged'." He tells who is going to sing *ganonhsagwende? owennui?ah,* "the empty [vacant] house of the deranged songs," and who will help him. "Then also someone will sing *ganonyahgwen?,* the round dance; his name is Haono?on."

Conductor II also tells who will wear the mask and impersonate *shagodyoweh,* the mask spirit. "He is named Gaiwagon:, 'Amidst the words.'"

Reply of the sponsor's spokesman (5): "I told them that Hawi?teon:k, ["Lodged in a fork (crotch)," Conductor I] would 'carry' the sponsor back and forth during *owennui?ah.* I also announced who would assist Conductor II in singing the round dance." They then commenced to pass the berry juice.

Figure 19 shows the floor plan for the "deranged songs" rite. The participants sing four songs seated, led by a singer of the opposite moiety (10). On the fourth song, they stand and take positions on the floor. A and B are polar positions in a shuttle between moieties. The song leader takes up his position at B, where he is joined by Conductor II (of moiety II), who is in charge of the ceremony. Meanwhile, across the fire, the sponsor has taken up her position at

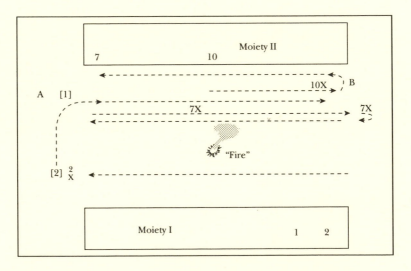

FIGURE 19. Floor plan and seating arrangement for the "deranged" or "hot" songs.

A, where she is joined by Conductor I, of her moiety, halfway
through the fourth song. At each repeat of a song thereafter, they
change ends. The sponsor and Conductor I pass between the seated
ranks of the two moieties and, at the midpoint of the shuttle,
between the oncoming singer and Conductor II. On the repeat they
pass back to their original positions. Thus, at the beginning of each
song, they are in their original positions.

Other singers join the song leaders as a chorus during the four
songs of passage. At the end of the fourth song, they all sit.

When the sponsor's speaker (5) announces this event, he says:
"They will take her back and forth [*ensagodiawiʔshonʔ*]" (fig. 20). When
someone is too ill to stand, a substitute stands in for the sponsor, an
act that is thought to help the sick person. My sources did not know
of carrying the sick person in the transit, except for small children.
Early sources indicate otherwise.

Intermission. Berry juice passed.

The sponsor's song: "She brightens the flame" (*deyehdohgwahgwa:t*).

FIGURE 20. The sponsor, Florence Crouse, and her conductor, Hiram
Watt, pause in passage between the singers. (WNF neg. 1940.II.57.)

Actually, her conductor sang two or three songs for her (*osagodja?don:dak,* "he sang for her"). This act initiates a period of "throwing songs" back and forth between individuals of opposite moieties—*waenondeno?ya:k.* I noted the following order: 2 vs. 12; 6 vs. 11; 5 vs. 10; 4 vs. 9; 3 vs. 8; 2 vs. 7. The alternation of singers proceeds from alternate ends of the facing benches, so that the song proceeds back and forth, rotating around the "fire" to the right. The individual songs appeal to familiars or tutelaries of the society and boast of magic power.

When Johnson Jimerson sang a particular song, both sides stood and danced. The text announced the entrance of crows:

1. *He djo gah ga:? dadi:yon?,* "Crows are coming in."
2. *He djo gah ga:? o?thadidat,* "they stand up."
3. *He djo gah ga:? o?thenon:,* "they dance."
4. *He djo gah ga:? sahennondjen:?,* "they sit down."

Johnson shared the Hawk clan with the sponsor, but the other moiety might perform this bit if they chose.

At the end of throwing songs back and forth across the fire, the lead singer of the opposite moiety (7) sang some four fast songs, although anyone might do this bit. My mentor did not deem songs personal property. He was not taught a song to sing but heard one, liked it, and now performed it. He regarded the repertoire as "free" songs. Likewise at Six Nations in Canada (according to Sherman Redeye and Clara Redeye).

Ganonyahgwen?, the round dance, follows immediately (figs. 21, 22). The first song is sung while seated. Then, led by Conductor II, Chauncey Johnny John, the singers—now dancers—circle closely around the fire between the benches, the leaders facing in, marching side-step and leaning toward the fire. They straighten up between songs. The two conductors put the sponsor between them and then circle the room around the benches.

Enter the masker. Just then the masker entered the door to the house used by visitors and joined the round dance at the end of the

FIGURE 21. The round dance, *ganonyahgwen?*. (WNF neg. 1940.II.58, Richard B. Congdon photo.)

FIGURE 22. The round dance. (WNF neg. 1940.II.59, Richard B. Congdon photo.)

line (fig. 23). Jonas Snow, of the sponsor's clan (Hawk), performed this role wearing a "Buffalo" mask by Richard Kettle of Cattaraugus. Jonas performed a jumping scissors step, as I observed, but I was later told that "the masker may dance any way he chooses." At the end of the dance cycle the masker went to the kitchen stove and blew ashes on the sponsor, for which service he received tobacco from the conductor. He departed by the door he had entered. Presently he returned unmasked for the feast.

The feast. Both conductors collected the invitation corn from their respective singers and returned it to the sponsor. ("She should have received the identical corn that she had from a previous feast, but she had lost it.") Once the corn is used at the initial feast, the patient must keep it for future renewals.

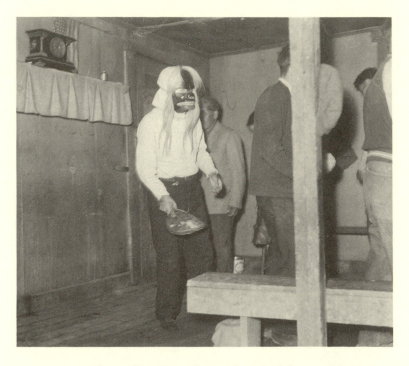

FIGURE 23. The masker enters during the round dance. (WNF neg. 1940.776.)

The women helpers appointed by the sponsor each gave a pan of pork chunks to the two conductors to distribute among the singers on their respective sides. All collections and distributions go counter-clockwise. Each conductor kept the bench on his right so that together they would make a counterclockwise circuit.

Passing half a hog's head, a conductor proclaimed, "Enswehe:k o:nenh wa?agwagahga? [let it be known now that we pick as crows]!" (fig. 24). This is *gahga?go:wa:* speaking. Persons present witness the singers eating like crows and crying *ga:? ga:?*.

Meanwhile, Conductor I, of the sponsor's moiety, ladled out the hulled corn soup in pails placed at random around the boiler in response to his cry, "Come set down your kettles [pails]." Having filled the pails, he cried, "Come, pick them up! [*donsa:jik*]."

For the man who had impersonated the masker, there was mush, which he dished out on the pail lids. Several persons ate it on the spot; others took it home.

"Ho: Pick up your pails and go home."

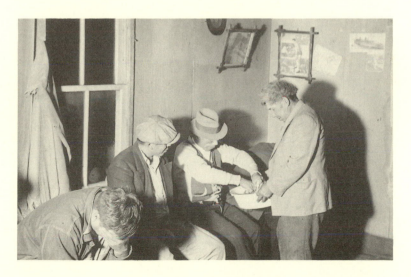

FIGURE 24. "We pick like crows": passing the pig's head. (WNF neg. 1940.II.61.)

❖ 7 ❖

Songs of the "Great Sharp Point"
Order of *I:ʔdo:s*

On February 13, 1941, at Coldspring Longhouse on the Allegany Reservation, Chauncey Johnny John, or Haunnoʔon (Turtle clan), with his grandson Richard Johnny John (Beaver clan) as second singer, recorded for the Library of Congress the songs of the "Great Sharp Point" order of *i:ʔdo:s* (William N. Fenton: records no. 49B–55B). Accompaniment: gourd rattles. These recordings comprise all of the songs of the ceremony performed in June 1940 for Florence Crouse that I observed and described with the help of Henry, Sherman, and Clara Redeye (chapter 6). My transcriptions of the song texts include comments by the singers.

This order of the great *i:ʔdo:s* ceremony is called the "Great Sharp Point" (*gayoweonʔgo:wa:h*) or, more familiarly, "going through the forest" (*hadihadi:yaʔs*). It consists of five parts or movements:

1. The marching songs of going through the forest (5)
2. The messenger's songs (11)
3. Throwing songs across the fire (individual songs) (10)
4. Middle or "deranged" songs for curing (10)

5. The round dance, *ganonyahgwenʔ,* or, in this more elaborate
   ceremony, *ganonyahgwenʔgo:wa,* which includes 12 songs
   addressed to the masker (approximately 64 songs in all).
Total: approximately 100 songs[1]

Two versions of the songs were current at Coldspring in the
1940s. Chauncey Johnny John grew up at Cattaraugus but in the
1890s moved to Allegany, where he had lived and worked for fifty
years. His version of the medicine society songs derived from
Benjamin Lewis of the Horseshoe settlement upriver and east of
Salamanca. George Jacobs had learned the Horseshoe version from
Lewis and brought it to Coldspring. Jacobs's wife, Sally, mother of
Alice White, matron of the Wolf clan in her seventies, taught the
songs to Chauncey at the same time she taught him the songs for
renewing the Little Water medicine. Chauncey then lived at Quaker
Bridge, where, he said, "Old George Jacobs's woman used to come
down from Coldspring: she liked to hear the spring frogs."

A second version then current at Coldspring among the middle
generation, who claimed it to be the authentic Coldspring variant,
derived from Frank Abrams, whose son Deforest, along with Lynn
Dowdy and Sherman Redeye, vouched that it was the correct one.
The late Clarence White sang it nearly correctly. It was said that
Sherman sang parts of three versions.

The Marching Songs: "Cutting through the Forest"

The traveling singers start at a neighboring house, but it as if they
were going through the forest to another town (cf. *Jesuit Relations* on
the Hurons).

---

1. The numbers of songs given here for the various parts come from informants'
statements and differ somewhat from the numbers recorded by Chauncey and Richard
Johnny John. Informants' statements and performances seldom agree precisely.

Introductory speech of the head raven, as leader of the medicine society and messenger (Record 49B, strip 1): "O:nenh engwahdandi gagwe:gon deswadenno:den? dentwa:tak [now we shall set out; all of you shall sing]." Songs:

1. *Gahganehe? dehahayondye: gahgane:* (repeat)
   "Raven approaches flying slowly."
   (This is the Great Raven's song as head of the medicine society.)

2. *Gahgane he?e: dahowen:no:t gahga:ne:* (repeat) *hai? yenh*
   "Raven's cry (voice) sounds afar; Raven."

3. *Gahgane he?e: wahogaini gahga:ne:* (repeat) *hai? yenh*
   "Raven enters (the lodge); Raven."

At the third song, the visitors enter the door, turn right, and pass before the waiting phratry of singers on their right. They turn left around the fire and stand before the empty bench where they are to sit. The first three songs are each repeated three times, sometimes as many as six times, before the visitors reach the door and enter. Then, standing before the empty bench, they sing:

4. *Wedzogahga wahadiyo:ne?* (repeat) *ha he:* (repeat) *hai? yenh*
   "The Ravens have arrived."

5. *Wedzogahga wahennonjenne ganonhshen?geh wahennodjenne: hai? he:*
   (repeat)
   "These Ravens are going to sit down in the middle of the house. They do sit."

At midsong, the visiting party sits down on the empty bench across the fire from the singers of the sponsor's moiety. The visiting headman says: "Ne?ho nowathgwe:ni? [there, that's the best we can do]."

The Messenger's Songs: *Hadjaswas hoenon?*

Less elaborate forms of *i:?do:s* include these same songs, which are repeated but once, the same tune throughout.

Record no. 50. The head messenger says: "O:nenh gwa:no engadeno:den? neh hadjaswas hoenon? enswazagon:? enswadenotak [right now, I shall sing the messenger's songs. Do your best to sing (with me) as well as you are able]."

1. *Owa?sawane: he?i he?i* (repeat three times)
   Wa?ahiya: hye:
   "Now it is starting."
   ("Now the hoot owl is coming," in the version of Sherman Redeye, who sings, *owa?dadawene:*. Halfway through the song, the company joins in.)

2. *Da?akdonne? he he?i:*
   Da?akdon? one? dadakhe? he?i:
   Da?akdon? dadakhe? one? he?i: (repeat)
   Wa?heya hyenh
   "He is coming to see,
   "He comes running to see."

3. *Dadkdonne he?e*
   (a) *wa?ahayon ne?i:*
   (a) (c) (d) (repeat)
   Wa?ashrya hyenh
   "He comes to look,
   "He has arrived."

4. *Dayosawadye: he?e e: he?e:*
   Dao?owadye: (b) (b)
   (a) (repeat) *wa?aheya*
   "It is beginning,
   "It commences from the beginning."
   (This means that the men who are sitting there will commence from the beginning and sing in rotation.)

5. *Waʔosawadye: heʔe: heʔe:* (repeat)
   (a) (repeat) *waʔaheya hyenh* (end)
   "It is going,
   "It has gone on to the next (song)."
   (They have begun the ceremony, and the lead has gone on to the next song.)

Record no. 50B, strip 1. Songs 6–9 parallel 4–7 of Sherman Redeye's version, in which the younger singer identified the text as "she is in a boat." Nevertheless, *enʔo:wenʔ* and *haʔo:wenʔ* refer to the female and male brant (small, dark-colored geese), which also appear in songs to renew the Little Water medicine (Group II, songs 11 and 12). Here again the songs run in pairs, female and male.

6. *Ye:i howen henʔen* (repeat three times)
   (a) (b) (a) (b) (repeat) *waʔaheya hyenh*

7. *Hahowenʔ henʔen*
   (a) (a) (b) (repeat) *waʔahiya hiya* (var. *hyenh*)
   "The male brant (*haho:wenʔ*)."

8. *Yehayohoʔo: yehayohoʔo:*
   Yei (a) (a) (repeat) *waʔahiya hyah*
   "Female brant is on the water."

9. *Hahonyohoʔo:* (etc.)
   "He, too, is on the water."

10. *Gahgane heʔehi*
   (a) *dadakhe heʔei*
   (a) *daʔadakhe heʔei* (repeat) *waʔaheya hyenh*
   "Raven that picks,
   "Raven is running this way (var., comes running)."

11. Same song, but substitute *waʔahoyone,* "he has arrived."
   "Raven that picks,

"Raven has arrived."
(Informants speak of the bird as a crow, although "Big Crow" or Raven is intended. Both species pick at carrion like crows. Participants imitate the birds at the feast.)</>

Record no. 51, strip 1. The last three messenger's songs:

12. *Yeda?akhe?i a dayeyin?on?o* (repeat)
    Yowi?i?i (c) (repeat)
    "She comes running, she enters."

13. *Aga?aden?en non gei en don?on?on*
    Yeidakheia dayeyon?on?on
    Yowi?i? (repeat three times) *hai? yenh*
    "I am trying with my song to help,
    "Who comes in running."
    (Speaking, *agadennon?geahdon?,* "I am trying with my singing [to help]"; *dayeyon?,* the one who comes in running. According to Chauncey, a woman is speaking who has entered running to help the person hosting the ceremony.)

14. *Wadehenhnon:denjon?ongo: gahi:donhon gaya:shon*
    (a) (repeat) *hai? yenh*
    "Release the songs of the ceremony
    "That is called *gahi:donhon* (or *i:?do:s*)."
    (In speech, *wade:nonhdenjon:go?,* "free the songs," which Chauncey said meant to commence, or free them for use. The messenger dumps the songs in the middle of the floor, just as he dumps out the rattles from a sack. *Gahi:donhon,* "sharp point," equates with *i:?do:s.*)

At the end of his last song, the messenger cries, "Ne?to: [that's enough]." Then he speaks:

Daonendi son nengen: honwe:gwa endwonsowen? endwano:den? nengen
So now then from the far end let us begin; we shall sing what-
ne?hodishon ganonhshen? o?gyeonto? ne? i:?do:s gae:non?

ever (of) in the middle of the house I dump the *i:ʔdo:s* songs.
ennohdon:ʔ gen:s neh ene:ʔ ne:ʔ gadeno:denʔ / da:neʔho.
It is up to him which one he shall chose to sing. That is all.

"Throwing Songs" by Individuals

Once the messenger has released the songs in the middle of the
lodge, then one after the other, beginning at the far end of his bench,
men speak and sing as the circuit goes counterclockwise around the
fire.

Record no. 51, strip 2. Each singer says, in effect, "At this time I
shall sing for the one who is sponsoring this ceremony that it may
help her."

First singer:
> *Da onendi onengwa:nonʔ engadeno:denʔ enkhenongohdenʔ nengen neh*
> *goyaʔdagwenniyoʔheonʔ*
> "So now then l sing for she who is sponsoring this ceremony that
> it may help her body."
> Song: *Haiyo haiyoʔo haiyo haiyoʔo ho:* (repeat) *haiyenh neʔto:*

Second singer (Richard Johnny John) (strip 3):
> *Da o:nenh di iʔne:waʔ engadeno:denʔ*
> "So now in my turn I shall sing."
> *Yoʔo heya ya* (repeat twice)
> *Wahongwainnoyenʔenʔ hik*
> (a) (a)
> (In speaking, *waʔhongwainoyenʔhik,* "we erred in the song," which
> is considered amusing.)

Third singer (strip 4, a short song):
> *O:nendagon ganon:ge: noʔowa:ʔ hai:yo:ʔo*
> "In the hemlocks are many owls." (repeat)
> "The hemlocks are full of hoot owls."
> Crowd: *Haiʔ yenh*
> Singer: *Neʔto:,* "that's all."

Crowd: *Nyoh,* "OK."
(This ending sequence follows the individual songs.)

Record no. 51B, strip 1:
Fourth singer (usual speech):

> *Hawei niyo: weniyoho* (repeat)
> *O?wadenonhdandi he?i,* "it is going on."
> *Gahidonhon gowa ha?a* (repeat), "the great *i:?do:s* ceremony."
> "The great ceremony of *i:?do:s* is going on (is in progress)."

When the last singer on the messenger's side has sung, he hands it over the fire to the bench of the sponsor.

Strip 2:
Fifth singer (CJJ):

> *Engidenste:? ne? tsoda:ge:?,* "woe is me, as I was coming,"
> *Hai he o?gya?dje:nen?,* "I fell down on the way."
> (b) *hai? he* (repeat) *hai? yenh*
> "Woe is me, as I was coming, I fell down on the way."</>

A member of the medicine society had the misfortune to fall down on the way to the meeting. A member coming late to the performance must enter singing like the others preceding him. This is considered something of a joke on the tardy shaman, especially if he does not know the marching songs of "cutting through the forest."

Strip 3:
Sixth singer (RJJ):

> *Heyo heyo yo?odjinnhe:* (nonsense vocables)
> *Hauhe heyo heyo*
> (b) *haihe*

Strip 4:
Seventh singer (CJJ):

> *Gagwegon gende?i heniyon,* "everyone I know of the,"
> *Wadinyo?o gagwegon gendehi,* "all the wild animals I know," etc.

Hai yoho wiyeh he?e?e (repeat)
Hai yeh: ne:?to:
(Apparently this is the boast of a shaman about his animal familiars.)

Record no. 51B, strip 5:
Eighth singer:

Dahadidak henon?ondje?e?e, "They come running,"
Hono:tcinohgen?, "the mystic animals,"
Hai?i he: dahadiha:gen?, "they emerge from the woods."
Hai?i he: (repeat) *hai? yenh*
Ne?to:
(In speech, *dahadidakhenondje?,* "they come running; the mystic animals of the medicine company come running out of the forest.")

A note on the manner of individual singing. Each man may sing more than one song. One song is the minimum, but the business of throwing songs may last quite a while. A good singer who knows several songs may, by alternating key words, make up a whole group of related songs. On a particular song, when he so declares, the singers of both benches will stand and dance, turning from side to side. Such songs concern various medicine animals and birds: brant, great raven (*gahga?go:wa:*), hoot owl, wolf, and muskrat. For example, Albert Jones (Snipe clan) sang a group on the theme "muskrat along the creek." This custom apparently derives from the old custom of singing songs praising one's animal familiars.

The Middle, or Curing, Songs

The middle songs (*gainowetahon*), or curing songs, are sometimes called "deranged" (*owenui?ah*). Among the Senecas at Coldspring, the messenger and his helper lead the songs comprising this group, which, according to Chauncey, is not sung at Six Nations. This group may be sung to release the Little Water medicine on the fourth night after a confinement. In this instance, the June 1940 ceremony described in chapter 6, the singers—Chauncey as messenger and Richard, his grandson—stood at the far end of the bench opposite the conductor for the sponsor (Hiram Watt) and the patient-sponsor (Florence Crouse), who stood across the fire diagonally opposite.

Halfway through the song, messenger and helper pass the other two, who go inside of them close to the fire to occupy the original position of messenger and assistant. The song is then repeated, and the two couples return in the same manner to their original positions.

The song sequence follows this pattern: each song is sung twice with the company. First, the lead singer, standing at his station, goes halfway; he repeats with the company, and the couples march. The sponsor and conductor always pass inside of the messenger and helper. The second time, the messenger sings halfway, standing at the other couple's station, but on the repeat, both couples return to their original positions. They must return to their original stations, I was told.

The ten songs were recorded halfway to save space. They resemble the marching songs of Part I.

Record no. 52, strip 1:
> Richard Johnny John, singer.
> Announcement: *Da o:nenh enwondennohdandi? neh gainonwetahon* "So now let the rite commence of the mid-songs." ("So now let the rite of the middle songs begin.")

1. *Ga?ahga ne? ei gahga?a ne? i*
   (a) *yohinenne:* (repeat)
   (a) (b) (repeat)
   "Raven Raven,
   "Raven *yohinenne,*
   "Raven *yohinenne.*"

2. *Da?adonkne?ee: dakdonne?ee: hi*
   (a) *yohinenhe* (repeat) *hai? yeh*

"He is coming to find out,
"He is coming to look."

3. Strip 3:
   Gaʔahenhenʔgeh nijawenonʔne:[2]
   (a) (b) *hai he:* (repeat) *haiʔ yeh*
   "Atop the tall timber,
   "Whence it came."

4. (Not recorded.)
   Ganonhsagon heyawenon ne:ʔ
   (a) (b) *neʔi*
   (a) (b) (c) (repeat) *haiʔ yeh*
   "In the lodge it has gone."

5. (Not recorded.)
   Ganonhsen:engeh heyawenon hei (repeat)
   "In the middle of the house,
   "It has gone (it went)."
   (At midsong the singers stand.)

6. Strip 4:
   Ganonhsenʔgeh hadehi:t
   Yaʔa heʔeʔe: hadehi:t
   Yaʔa hadehi:t
   Yaʔa heʔeʔeʔeh
   Hadehi:t yaʔa (repeat) *hai*
   "Midway of the lodge
   "They stand."

Here the messenger and helper, who stand at one end of their bench, and the conductor and the sponsor, standing diagonally across the fire at the end of their bench, go back and forth at midsong, the conductor and sponsor passing between the messenger and helper.

------

2. *Gaʔahenhenʔgeh,* "atop the tall timber" in archaic Seneca, becomes *gaʔengenye:t* in modern Seneca, referring to "treetops."

Strip 5:

7. *Godegiya godegi:*
   Ya?a he?e:i godegiya
   (c) (b)
   (c) *he?e?e?i*
   (c) (a)
   (a) (repeat)
   (A female song of nonsense vocables sung first when sponsor is of that gender.)

8. *Hodegiya,* etc.
   The male counterpart of seven.
   (In Sherman Redeye's version, this pair is also 7 and 8, but he interprets the two as meaning, "Something of hers [his] burns." Whether this refers to the patient's passing back and forth near the fire remains uncertain.)

9. Strip 6:
   Yohinene ha?igen: ne?i
   (b) (c) (a) (repeat)

10. *Yowinenne ne?e: ha?inen: ne?i*
    (b) (c) (a) (repeat)
    Hoga?anon?onsayen? endaje?e:
    Hainen: ne: he yohinen:ne (repeat) *hai yenh*
    Singer: *Dane?ho,* "that is all."
    ("He/she travels house to house" [in speech, *hoganonhsayendadye?*]. In modern times, "He/she travels the length of the house." Evidently in ancient times, the rite passed through the fires of several longhouses, as in Huronia, according to the *Jesuit Relations.*)

The same tune obtained through song 8; songs 9 and 10 are again female and male. Only song 10 was recorded.

Informants differed on the meaning of the text in songs 9 and 10. Although Chauncey Johnny John and his grandson Richard, who recorded the songs, favored "through the houses" or "the length of a single longhouse," as indeed one may observe of participants in the ceremony, Sherman Redeye explained the ninth and tenth songs of his version, which are *hoʔganonhsayenda:jeʔ haʔdehi:t,* as meaning "there in the far end of the house they two [she/he] are standing." In his view, the dual form of "standing" referred to the patient and the conductor of her moiety, who stand together.

The first two songs of this rite were omitted from our recording because they are sung as a preface to this section when releasing the medicine from a patient at the end of his confinement. They are as follows:

1. *O:nenh hosayondataʔ*
   "Now he releases you."

2. *Onenh onenh*
   Heʔtgen heʔtgenh
   Hosayondataʔ hosayondataʔ
   "Now now,
   "High up overhead,
   "He puts you away."

It is the practice of medicine bundle holders to hide their medicine bundles under the rafters, a practice that apparently derives from the old Iroquois custom of storing things overhead under the eves, on the shelf over a man's bunk in the communal longhouse.

The Round Dance

The round dance that concludes the Great Sharp Point ritual is called *ganonyahgwenʔ* or, in complete form, *ganonyahgwenʔgo:wa:,* the "Great Medicine Dance," or, less frequently, "the high song," *heʔtgen nigainonʔe:ʔ.*

Record no. 52B. To save space, Chauncey sang but halfway through the songs, which are ordinarily twice the recorded length.

Strip 1. The singer announces, "Endwainongaida:t o:nenh [let us begin the song now]." Ten or eleven songs are sung while seated

(Chauncey said sixteen); then six or seven are sung standing, followed by the round dance.

1. *Yowinehe hegahennon* (repeat)
    (a) (b) *gwaʔ gwahe:* (ending cry)
    (Speaking, *neh gainonʔ,* "the song," becomes [a] singing.)

2. *Gahidohon oʔwadennonhdandiʔ hi*
    Howadenonhdandi hi hi (repeat) *gwaʔ gwahe:*
    "*I:ʔdo:s* ceremony has begun,
    "It is under way."

3. *Ha ie haʔiye*
    Higen higen (repeat) *heʔe hen*

4. *Gahidonhon age:gen neʔ huiweʔhe: neʔ gaenonʔ* (repeat)
    "*I:ʔdo:s,* I see it walking, the song,
    "I see the song of *i:ʔdo:s,* it is walking."

5. *Gahidohon age:gen neʔ huiweʔhe: hewage:nonʔ*
    "On seeing the song of *I:ʔdo:s* walking, I went there."

6. *Yowine gaʔayaha:* (three times and repeat)

7. *Yowine gaʔayoʔoʔo yohoʔoʔoh*
    Heʔe he: hojiha hawine
    Hayo:: yo::haʔa (repeat)

8. *Yowine gaʔayoʔoʔo yohoʔoʔoh*
    Heʔe he: jodaha hawine
    Hayo: yo: hoʔ (repeat)

9. *Yoho johennaga dadiyon yoho* (repeat)[3]
    "Yonder song they (animals) come in."

---

3. *Joennaga: dadiyon:,* "distant song, they come in." Animals hear the song at a distance and come where the song is being sung.—CJJ.

10. *Yoho johennaga dadiyon yoho*
    Yoho jongwayon yoho
    Yaho yogo (repeat)
    "Hearing distant song, we came in here,
    "Hearing yon song, we arrived here."

11. *Okensen okensenhen hoganonhsayendadye?[4] yowione:* (repeat)
    "They are stomping the entire length of the longhouse."

Singers arise:
12. *Do:di do:di dwadennongehehat* (repeat)
    "Let us try,
    "Let us try to help."
    (At this song the singers all stand [*hadi:dat*] and pledge to help
    the sick person: *dwadennon?gea:t,* "let us try to help her.")

Record no. 53. The round dance. The company remains standing
still while singing until the participants begin to dance around the
room at song 17.

13. *Ohdendjon ha?a?a hai de* (repeat) *ne?ho gagehenon* (repeat)
    Gwa? gwa? he:
    "It is moving, this my song."

14. *O?jongwanon sohi:den? hai he?* (repeat)
    "We fill the house with noise of stomping."
    (*O?jongwanonhsahi:den?,* "we the house fill with noise of stomp-
    ing" [Sherman Redeye's song 9].)

15. *?Ohden:jon* (repeat) *ne?ho o?jongwaya?dendonson?*
    "It is going; here we turn our bodies side to side."
    (The singers pretend to dance.)
    "We are stirring."

16. (a) (repeat) (b) *o?jongwagonhsendonson* (repeat)

---

4. "They are stomping, stomping the length of the house."

"We turn our faces side to side,
"We peer about."

17. (a) (repeat) (a) (repeat)
    "It is going, moving, it has started."
    (Here, where the tempo increases, they begin to dance.)

Dancing songs. The singer, standing, cries *gwa? he:?*, and the company, standing, responds before and after each song. Songs 18–23 are variations of same tune.

Strip 2:
   18. *We?enniyo henhen* (twice and repeat)

   19. *Ha?enniyo henhen* (repeat)
       Hainiyo henhen (repeat)

   20. *Gwen?eniyo henhen* (repeat)
       Gwenniyo henhen (repeat four times)

   21. *Wen enniyo henhen* (repeat)
       Wen:niyo henhen (repeat)

   22. *Ha?iwiyo henhen* (repeat)

   23. *Ha?ehiyo henhen* (repeat)

Record no. 53B, strip 1 (the next series has long words):
   24. *Gwa? gwahe:*
       Hogaya: hogoyaha ha?a (end)
       Deyongwahen hennongohdon?on (repeat from the beginning)
       "We have performed the songs."
       (*Deyongwaenongohdon*, "We have performed the songs." The company has sung in rotation its individual songs.—CJJ)

   25. *Gwa? gwa he:*
       Hogaya hogaya ha?a (repeat) (end)

Djongwahenhenʔ nongesgwen
(a) (a) (repeat from the beginning)
"We have repeated the song."
(*Dejongwaenonge'sgwen,* "we repeated the song." We have reached
the midpoint of the songs and repeated.—CJJ)

26. *Hogaya hogaya hasʔa*
     Dejongwadonhen jongohdonʔon
     "We passed through narrow valleys."
     (*Dejogwadoendzogohdoʔ,* "we narrow valleys [*dyoehdi*] passed
     through." When they arrived [marching through the forests],
     they came through valleys and over hills [as if one village were
     journeying to the relief of another]. "We came through ravines."
     In Sherman Redeye's song 10, "They came through the earth.")

27. *Hogoya hogoya haʔa*
     Waha:ʔa waha:ʔa nehi (dancers stagger)
     Otadiyaʔa dodadiyeʔionʔon
     (a) (a)
     "All their bodies are swaying,
     "Both phratries are swaying."
     (*Otadiyaʔdondadyeiʔsonʔon,* "on both sides their bodies are sway-
     ing." The whole company of singers, both moieties, dance, sway-
     ing their bodies. The singers stagger, swaying side to side as they
     dance. At this point the songs get mixed, as individual singers
     order the sequence differently, which happens frequently in rit-
     ual. Then the song leader has to commence over so that they are
     all singing in unison.)

28. *Sayoden:ʔ sayoʔondon: hai he* (repeat)
     "Woman, you are lucky, you will recover."

29. *Watcondon watconʔondonʔ hai he* (repeat)

30. *Iʔgendeʔe iʔgendeʔe hi hi*
     Waʔagononhonkdenʔ
     (a) (a) (repeat) *gwaʔ gwahe:*
     "I know, I know,

"She did get sick,
"I know, I know."
(*I?gende? wa?agononkden?*, "I know that she did get sick.")

31. *Wa?kejen?nh wa?kejjen?nh hen?en*
     I?gende?e ho:dajeshon?on
     "I make her well,
     "I know that [I have the power],
     "I know I can cure her."

Record no. 54A:

32. *Gwa? gwahe:*
     Hayon?wa hayon?wahon
     Yohige:gen yowigegen hen: (repeat)

33. *Ha?yonwo: ha?yonwon:*
     Hai?ge?gen haiheh haihe (repeat from the beginning)

34. *Hojigengen hojigengenhen*
     Jigen?gen?gen?he
     (a) (a) (a) (a) (repeat) (Sherman Redeye's song 39.)

35. *Ho? gainondiyondon nongwaenon*
     Ha?yon?we hi higen?ne
     Ha?yon?we ha?yonwahi?yo (repeat)
     "Our song is mixed (confused)."
     (Our singing is in opposition. The next song states the same
     thing, but with longer words. There follows a series of songs
     with short, then longer words.)

36. *Hegahenondiyonden:? nongwa?henno?genon?ho:* (repeat)
     Gwa? gwahe:
     "Our songs are clashing."

37. *Yowihi yo?owihi*
     Gahi?daniyondon?hon: (repeat)
     "The *i:?do:s* ceremony is hung up (overhead)."

38. *YoʔowihÍ yoʔowihi ne yo:owihi*
    HenʔEn: gahiʔdaniyondonʔhon
    (a) (a) (b) (a) (repeat)
    "The *i:ʔdo:s* ceremony is hung away."

39. *YoʔO ho: ganesagon neʔhoʔi:weʔ*
    WeʔEyoho (a) (a) (repeat)
    "Beneath the hillside
    They are walking."

Record no. 54B:
40. *Jihondo:den jihondo:denhen*
    Gado:gen gadogenhen
    "They stand up a twig (tree),
    "In a certain place."

41. *Jihondo:den jihondo:denhen*
    GanoʔshEn ganoʔshenhen (repeat)
    "They stand up a twig,
    "They erect a tree,
    "In the middle of the lodge,
    "In the middle of the lodge."
    (Here the dancers pretend to stand their rattles on end several
    feet above the floor.)

42. *Gwaʔ gwahe:*
    (a) (a) *ehdaʔgeha hahondenhowihi* (repeat)
    "They erect a limb (timber),
    "Low down he is carrying it."
    (Here the dancers reach down low and plant their rattles in the
    center of the lodge.)

43. *Gwaʔ gwahe:*
    Waʔkhenyodenʔ waʔkhenyodenʔhen
    Gado:gen gado:genhen
    "I stood her up, I stood her up,
    "In a certain place,
    "In a certain place."

44. *Gwaʔ gwahe:*
    Ganonhshen ganonhshenhen (repeat)
    Gwaʔ gwahe:
    "I stood her up,
    I stood her up,
    In the center of the lodge,
    In the center of the lodge."
    (If the patient is a man, the male pronominal form of the verb is used. This song alerts the patient to stand, ready to go around in the dance.)

45. *Gwaʔ gwahe:*
    Waʔhaʔa waʔhaʔa nehe keyadenonhgeadonʔ (repeat)

46. *Doʔodi doʔodihi keyahdenjedohonʔ* (repeat)
    "I will try to have her dance,
    "I will try to make her go."
    (She does not dance yet, but stands still in the middle of the room while the company dances around her—RJJ. Sherman Redeye sings this in the dual form, referring to both moieties. "Here she starts dancing."—SR)

Record no. 55:
47. *Hoʔtgainongondajeʔ hoʔttgaingonda:jehe* (repeat)
    "The last song (for the whole company),
    "The final song."
    (The cue for the man who will wear the mask to go outside and get ready to enter masked.)

Songs for the mask:
48. *Hojigengenh hojigengenhenh dehadigonhsaʔheʔah* (repeat)
    "The mask looks in."
    (The spoken term *dehadigonhsaʔheʔa* derives from *dethadiyonhsaʔha:ʔ,* "the mask looks in." Compare *dehadigonhsaʔhe:taʔ,* "the mask is shouting," SR's song 40.)

49. (a) (a) *dehanonnyayendonnehe*

"He comes dancing,
"They come dancing."

50. *Ojistagweniyondonhon*
    Waʔahe: waʔaha nehe (repeat) *wahe:*
    "Embers are ready,
    "She is saying."

51. *Ojistagweni deyoditha?* (repeat)
    Hennondonyonhon hon? on? on?
    "Live embers are ready,
    "They two say to each other."
    (The antiphonal consists of the nasal speech of two False Faces conversing.)

52. *Gwa? gwa he: hon? on? on?*
    (Singer; masker replies, *hai he: he?i hai he: he?i.* Singer first time; together on repeat of whole song.)
    Deyadigonhsane:gen (repeat)
    "Their two faces (mask and man) are together (vis-à-vis)."

53. *Gwa? gwa he:*
    Hai he he?e (repeat) (singer and later helper and company)
    Deyagigonhsa?ne:gen (repeat)
    "Our two faces are vis-à-vis (mask and sick person)."

54. *Hai he he?i* (repeat) (singer and later company)
    Dehinonhsa?ne:gen (repeat) (singer and company on repeat)
    "Their two faces are vis-à-vis."
    (Mask does not yet blow ashes.)

Record no. 55B:
55. *Gwa? gwa he:*
    Onen?yai (repeat) *hai he gwa? gwa he:*
    "Fire (hot stones)."
    (Literally, "a cooked stone." "Hot stones" is the masker's term for "fire." Other singers [SR no. 42] assert that the term refers to "heated stones" that the masker will juggle.)

56. *Hai he hei* (helper) *hai he hei*
    Singer: *O?dagwen ho?daagwen* (repeat)
    "Ashes flying about."
    (*O?da?geondagwen*, "flying ashes," as the masker tackles the fire pit.)

57. *Hai he hei* (helper replies)
    Wacistayenonda:non (repeat)
    Company: *Hai he hei*
    "Sparks are streaking."
    (Coals from the fire streak through the air.)

58. *Hai he hei* (repeat)
    Ha?tgonhsayanonda'non
    Hai he hei (by company first time)
    "He turns his face from side to side."
    (The masker goes to the fire and turns his face from side to side rapidly. His movements are quick.—CJJ)

59. Singer: *Hai he hei* (repeated by helper and company)
    Masker: *Hon? ?on ?on*
    Odidwahennonwehent gahido?ongowahaha?a
    "Let us put the songs overhead of the great *gahi:don* (*i:?do:s*) ceremony."
    (From the archaic form *odidwahennonwehen:t*, "let us the songs put overhead," which in modern Seneca becomes *odidwaennonwen: engawen:t*, "to put something up overhead.")

60. Singer: *Hai he hei* (repeated by company)
    Masker replies: *Hon? ?on ?on*
    Odiwahennonwehent gayoweo?on gowaha?a
    "Let us put away overhead the songs of the Great Sharp Point ceremony."

61. *Hai he hei* (repeat; usual response)
    Onenh sawahdendi?a? a
    Hai he hei nongwaenon?geon?

Hai he hei gahidohongowahaʔa
Gwaʔgwahe:
"Now he has departed (*sawahdandiʔa*),
"Our songs that are dead past
"Of the great *i:ʔdo:s* ceremony."

62. *Hai he hei* (repeat)
    In chorus: *Hai he hei o:nenh sawahdendiʔa*
    Hai he hei gahidonhongowaheʔa
    Hai he hei gayoweonʔongo:wa
    "Now it has gone home (away),
    "The great *i:ʔdo:s* ceremony,
    "The Great Sharp Point."

63. *Hai he hei dewano yayeondonʔnaʔs*
    "They have nearly finished dancing."
    (This is the last dance song, which refers to the masker's looking about for the patient before departing.)

64. Whole company in chorus: *Yohaha hei* (repeat)
    deganongeodaʔdyeshon
    "The horned ones butt each other."
    (The masked dancer has horns [antlers]. Here the dancers bow and put their rattles up to their heads like antlers, turn, and pretend to butt each other like bison.)
    Gwaʔ gwa he: gwaʔ gwa he:
    Ne:tho, "that's it."

Snatches of "Shake Pumpkin" at Tonawanda, 1936

While recording Seneca song styles at Tonawanda with Martha Champion Huot in May 1936, Chief Edward Black (Hawk clan), whom Corbett Sundown, his clansman, later succeeded in the conduct of the medicine company rituals, recorded snatches of the *i:ʔdo:s* songs (Record 36A, Huot and Fenton Collection, Archives of Traditional Music, Indiana University).

The singer remarked that one should use a gourd rattle to accompany these songs, but the texts become clearer without it.

The rite has no introduction, unless its performance represents the first transfer from a cure by the medicine to the celebration group, which is called *hadi:ʔdo:s honontcinohgenʔ*. After taking the medicine, the patient must use *gai:ʔdon* (put up a feast for the celebration group) even before she is able to get up and go around.

The *gai:ʔdon* ritual:

1. *Gahidohon enyeyaʔdak*, "i:ʔdo:s she must sponsor"
   Nen dyensonʔonni, "that she be able to go about"
   Yohenzageh yo:ndoni, "on earth that what she says"
   Hoʔ yagongwe, "that woman"
   Hoʔ haihoyoʔo haiʔ yenh

2. *Nidewehéʔ oʔtgon haigwa*, "I never thought it was so powerful"
   Gahidoʔohon wiye haiʔ yenh, "this sharp point ceremony"

3. *Dzothayoni haye:nons*, "the Wolf catches"
   Deyodinonʔgeon:donʔon, "creatures of whorling horns (sheep)"
   Haiʔ yenh
   (The melody resembles that of Period I of the all-night songs.)

4. *Hewagenon hedjonhehoʔ*, "I have been to the sky"
   Gayasonʔonne wiʔiyo::, "that is its name: it is beautiful (cornstalk)"
   Gayeheʔe gayeheʔe haiʔ yenh

5. *Deyonkgiga:ne:' neʔho*, "they are looking this way"
   Wenongwe deyonkni, "the women are looking"
   He: henʔenʔenʔen haiʔ yenh

APPENDIX A

The Tobacco-Burning Invocation for *Hadihadi:ya?s*

Following the ceremony outlined in chapter 6, Henry Redeye, then principal speaker at Coldspring Longhouse on Allegany Reservation of the Seneca Nation, dictated the text of the tobacco-burning invocation in his home near Quaker Bridge, with his son Sherman and Sherman's wife, Clara, acting as editor and interpreter, respectively. These persons have since gone the long trail.

I print here the English translation and refer the reader to the published Seneca text (Fenton 1980: 3–8).[1]

> So now the tobacco smoke arises at this time of night.
> So now he has furnished us with things that he [the Creator] ordained for people to use [the feast food, etc.]; they will utilize it as he has provided it.
> So this he himself has done: some people will continue to use it as he himself ordained that some people will continue to hear wherever [the message] is directed, as many of them as hear it.

---

1. My debt to Wallace Chafe for editing the Seneca text is enormous.

So now we will direct it to the very place where you are [met], members of this medicine society.

So now indeed you are the first, who are called "Big Crow," or Raven, for you volunteered to spread the message wherever there are members who remember [to honor the animal tutelaries]. So now then it is your responsibility to notify people to come assemble here.

So now you partake of the tobacco, you who cooperate, regardless of size, who are running about on the earth, all over wherever there are thickets, [where people do not go], and everywhere along the creeks, wherever there are dirty things in the streams [wherever there are pollutants in the streams].

So now therefore they partake of the tobacco.

So now you also cooperate who fly about high above the earth. And particularly that one who goes high above the clouds and beyond [Dew Eagle]. You do work together.

Therefore let them enjoy the tobacco.

So now everything is fulfilled, so let them enjoy the tobacco, as many as cooperate in the place where you will select to carry it, where you will enjoy the tobacco. So you will carry it to where one named Gada:thon? ["a taut line"] is.[2]

So she has fulfilled what you said should be ready: she will remember us [the mystic animals] by first setting down tobacco for us [in a twined corn-husk tray]. Accordingly, she has done it, she has set down the tobacco for us.

So now moreover she has provided this with which they will thank each other, the proper berry juice.

So now then the smoke arises, it will make you hear what she has fulfilled.

So now also you said a feast shall continue to be set down properly, which she also has ready, having pulled forth [procured] what used to move around close to the ground, what is called the "tame bear" [old name of pig], whose snout protrudes, which she has provided to pass around the fire when they finish the ceremony.

---

2. Name of person sponsoring the ceremony, from the Hawk clan roster.

So now the smoke arises by which you will hear.

She has fulfilled everything, by setting down a kettle of corn soup, all of which has been done that she shall thank them when they finish the ceremony.

So now the smoke is rising with which you will hear.

So now she has fulfilled everything. Now you are responsible [it is up to you] to do what you are capable of to enable her to pass through this sickness, which is windborne. And so she pleads that it will surely happen that she will pass through. So now also you all can intervene in this accident, which may occur anywhere on the earth. She pleads that surely it may happen that you can intervene.

So now moreover you have demonstrated that you are able to help this person who is helping herself; it won't be severe because she is helping herself by sponsoring this ceremony.

So now at this juncture you have stated that you can bring it back [retrieve them] even when their legs are hanging over the edge of the earth [grave].[3]

And so it shall be as the Creator ordained.

Therefore you are responsible [it is up to you] now that she has accomplished what you said should be done.

So now another thing that you have done, they are called our grandparent, you who come from toward the sunset [Thunders], you said that we shall carry tobacco [persons attending the meeting bring tobacco for the invocation].

So now you shall savor the tobacco, that you will restore the person of this your grandchild, for surely this will happen this time the way they plead for it, because of your great power to help people.

And now another thing, how her luck will be in her goings and comings because of the Great False Face.

So now you shall savor the tobacco, that one who is called *shagojowehgo:wa:h,* it shall be done that you shall come and go at the end of the ceremony. So it is proper that tobacco has

---

3. The medicine company can raise her up after she is so sick that her feet hang over the edge of the grave.—CR

been set down for you, and is also proper she has provided this kettle of mush that you favor, which is sweetened with bear grease.

So now then it is your responsibility, for you have great power, you can intervene in cases of sickness, whenever she pleads that it happen this way, since she is helping herself, and you can intervene in an accident.

And so now also the tobacco is savored, whatever kind of medicine you have, which he ordained for you to have used, and he intended that embers would be here on earth for the great masker to scoop up hot ashes from the fire.

So now then partake of the tobacco.

Therefore you are responsible in the future.

Dane?ho ["that's it"].

Henry then added the following "appendix" to his prayer, referring to the medicine dance itself:

So now this shares the tobacco, the *i:?do:s* song, this part that is called *oenhui?ah* ["deranged"] also partakes of the tobacco, and also this *ganonyahgwen?go:wa:h* ["great medicine dance"], which will be performed [so that] the medicine society members may enjoy it; it partakes of the tobacco.

So now another thing shares the tobacco, the rattle that strengthens your song.

So therefore this is the final word; this is your responsibility in the future [to maintain the ceremony].

Dane?ho. That is all.

APPENDIX B

Gertrude Kurath's Song Transcriptions and Scores

In a comprehensive study of Iroquois music and dance, the late Gertrude Prokosch Kurath (1964), of a musical family and herself an accomplished modern dancer, transcribed the recordings I made for the Library of Congress of the Coldspring version of *hadi:ʔdo:s,* or the medicine dance, as sung by Chauncey and Richard Johnny John (see chapter 7). In what follows, I reproduce Kurath's concise analysis of the medicine company, or society of shamans (1964: 11–12), which affords an abstract of the ceremony; her transcriptions of the song texts; and her musical scores for the songs (Kurath 1964: 132–38). The edited texts of sixty-four songs (see chapter 7) may be applied to reproducing the musical scores.

Medicine Company of Society of Shamans
(*hadiíʔdos* or *yeiʔdos*)

Function.—Cure, particularly to release the medicine administered to a patient in the Little Water Medicine ritual.

Occasions.—Usually in secret at night in the patient's home, infrequently during medicine rite renewals of Midwinter Festivals; at special meetings three times a year—June, September, and at Midwinter.

Songs.—(*a*) Marching songs of hadi'hadiya's or gahadiyá'gǫ "going through the forest," 5 songs, by entire company of 12 to 15 men all shaking gourd rattles (I). Slow, free delivery of ingeniously combined "Scotch snap" and triplet figures, in a scale of five to eight notes range, with rattle tremolo.

(*b*) Messenger's songs, 15 songs in groups of twos and threes (II). Free combinations of even notes, syncopations, and triplets, in narrow range scales of five tones, with rattle in triple time against duple time of melodies.

(*c*) Throwing songs or individual songs, any number, eight recorded (III). Solos by individual singers, in a great variety of tonalities and patterns, containing from 3 to 6 notes of the scale, with a range of 4 notes to 12, with repetition of the same short phrase triplets in a descending scale (1) or free phrasing (3).

(*d*) Middle songs (gainǫwé'tahǫ) or Curing songs, 10 songs by the Messenger and helper (IV). Groups of two or three songs, all constructed on a similar theme, stated in the first song, similar in tonality and rhythm to the Marching songs, but with a preference for an octave's range. Each song rendered twice, with alternation of rattle tremolo and even duple beat.

(*e*) Round dance, ganónyahgwɛ', 64 songs by the entire company (V), many of them in pairs. Triplets and syncopation in play on confined melodies, mostly of three tones encompassing four to five notes in thirds and seconds, the last song with fourths. Usually five repeats, with tremolo during first and fourth repeat.

Dance and ritual action.—(*a*) (part I) Marching from an adjoining house to ritual site.

(*b*) (part II) and (*c*) (part III) in place.

(*d*) Curing ritual by the following participants (part IV):

Messenger

Patient

Sponsor

Helper

Crossover during first rendering of each song; return to original places during second rendering.

(*e*) (part V) Round dance in three phases:

    i.   In place, seated, 11 songs, with rising during twelfth.

    ii. Standing, 5 songs.

iii. Dancing by the assembly, songs 18–47; by the sponsor and a masked figure, songs 48–55, ashes strewn; by the assembly, songs 56–62; in place, standing, final songs 63–64.

Step—facing center of circle, a sidward stamping shuffle and raising of alternate knees, sometimes a quick two-step or two successive stamps with one foot.

Actions:

41: rattles stood on end of handle several feet above floor.

42: rattles planted in center of dance lodge.

52–54: masker and sponsor face to face like two people kissing, ashes strewn by the masker.

63: rattles held against head like horns during butting mime.

Remarks.—Textual references to mystic animals and magical actions. Ordinary clothes except for black and white mask. Relation to even more esoteric Little Water Medicine Society.

Society of Shamans

TEXT AND TRANSLATION

I. Marching Songs (paired)—

  1. gahgahneehe'dehahayǫ' dye gahganee (repeat) hai yeh
        raven   approaches flying slowly   the raven

  2. gahgahne he'ee dahowɛɛnoot gahganee   hai yɛh
        raven   cries afar (his voice sounds)   (he is coming)

  3. gahghahne wahogaini haghanee   hai yek
        enters   raven

  4. wedzogahga wahadiyǫ'ne'   hai he   hai'yeh
        the ravens   they have arrived

  5. wedzogahga wahɛnodjɛne ganǫhshɛ'geh wahɛnodjɛnee hai he
      these ravens are going to sit down; in the middle of the house   they sit

  6. (At midsong all sit on the empty bench opposite the sponsor's moiety. The leader says, [ne'ho nowath' gweni," "there that's the best we can do.)

II. Messenger's Songs—(hajas'was hoe'nǫ')

  7. owa'sawɛnee he'i he'i
      now they are starting (hoot owl is starting)

8. da'akdǫne'   he he'ee   da'akdǫ'ǫne'   he'ii . . .
   he is coming to see   he comes running to see
   wa'aheya hyɛhɛ

9. dakdǫne   he'i   wa'ahayǫ neii: wa'aheya hyɛh
   he comes to see   he has arrived

10. dayosawadjee   he'e . . .   dayo'osawadjee   wa'ohoya
    it is beginning   it is starting from the beginning
    (The men sitting there will sing in rotation.)

11. wa'osawadjee   he'ee . . .   wa'osawadjee   wa'ahiha
    it is going   it has gone on to the next

12. yeei howɛ   hɛ'ɛ (3 times) (repeat all)   wa'ahiya hiya
    female duck

13. hahowɛ'   hɛ'ɛ . . .
    male duck [brant]

14. ye hayoho'oo   yeihayoho   yehayo ho'oo   wa'ahiya hiya
    female duck on the water

15. ha hoyo ho'oo . . .
    male duck on the water

16. gahgane   he'ei   gahga'ane   dadakhe   he'ei   wa'ahiya   hiya
    raven that picks   raven is running this way

17. gahgane   he'ei   gahgane   wa'ahayǫne   he'ei
    raven that picks   raven has arrived

18. yeda'akhe'i a   deyeyǫ'ǫ'ǫ   yowi'i'i . . .   haiyeh
    she arrives running   she enters running

19. aga'adɛ'ɛnǫ geiɛdǫ'ǫ'ǫ   yeidakheia dayeyǫ'ǫ'ǫ
    I am trying with my sǫng   she cǫmɛs ın runnıng

20. wadehɛ' nǫǫdɛdjǫ'ǫgoo   gahi'dǫhǫ gaya'shǫ   haiyeh
    let the songs commence   yeidos   it is called
    (Free the songs)

III. Throwing or Individual Songs—

1. haiyio haiyo'o . . . .   hai'yɛhɛne'too
   enough (that's all)

2. yo'o heya ya (repeat)   wahǫgwainnoyɛ' ɛ' hik (repeat)
   we made an error in the song

3. oonɛ'dagǫ   ganǫǫgee   no'owaa'   haiiyoo'o yahoo
   In the hemlocks are plenty of owls.

Crowd: hai'yɛh   Singer: ne'too   Crowd: nyoh

4. hawei niyoh weniyo   owadɛnǫhdändi he'i   gahidǫhǫh gowa ha'a
    It is going on   the great yeidos ceremony

5. ɛgidɛstee' ne'tsǫdaagee'   hai he o'gyajeenɛ'   ne'tsǫdaagee hai he
    Woe is me, as I was coming   I fell down as I was coming
    (An explanation of tardiness)

6. heyo heyo yo'ojinahee   haihe heyo heyo

7. gagwegǫ gɛnde'hi'i heniyǫ wadi'nyo'o   gagwegǫ gɛnde'hii
    Everyone I know of all the wild animals, everyone I know
    haii yo'ho wiyɛ hɛhɛ'ɛ'ɛ haiyeh   nee'too

8. dahadidak henǫ'ǫje'e'e   honǫǫčingǫhɛ'   hai'ihee dahadihaag'ɛ't
    They come running   the medicine company   they emerge from the woods
    hai'ihee   haiyeh   ne'too hai he

In counterclockwise rotation, each man speaks and renders his song. If he knows
a series, he may render several. The songs may concern animals, as the duck
(ɛǫwɛ), great raven (gahgagoowa), wolf (thayoni), hoot owl (o'owa'a), muskrat
(jinodaga). At his behest, all may arise and dance, turning from side to side.
Opposite moieties sit across the fire.

IV. Curing Songs (ow nui'ah)—

1. ga'abga ne'ei (repeat) yohinɛnee (repeat all)
    Raven, raven

2. da'adǫkne'ee   dakdǫne'e hi
    He is coming to find out; he is coming to see
    da'adǫkne'ee   yǫhinɛhe   hai'yeh

3. ga'ahɛhɛ'geh nija'weno'nee' (repeat)   hai hee   hai'yeh
    Atop the tall timbers whence it came

4. ganǫhsagǫ   heyawenǫ
    in the house   it has gone

5. ganǫhshɛ'ɛgeh   heyawenǫ
    in center of house   it has gone

6. ganǫhshɛgeh   hadehiit   ya'a he'eee . . . hai
    At the center of the lodge they stand

7. (Female song)—rendered first if the sponsor is a woman.
    godegiya godegiya   ya'a he'e'e'i godegiya ya'a he'e he'e'i

8. (Male song)—rendered first if the sponsor is a man.
    hodegiya . . . . .

9. hoga'anǫ'yɛ' ǫsayɛ' ɛndadje'eee   hainɛ'ɛ nee he yohinɛ'ne
    He travels house to house, the whole length of the longhouse

haiyεh   dane'hóh
    that's all

Note.—Two preliminary songs, to release Little Water Medicine, not included.

V.   Round Dance—(ganonyahgwen?go:wa)
    (Seated)
    1. yowinehe hegahεnọ (repeat)   gwa'a gwahee'
            the song
    2. gahidohọ o'wadεnọ'   hgeäat'hi   howadεnóhdändi hi hi
            yeidos ceremony is going on   it is going on
    3. haine ha'inε   higε higε   hε'εhε   gwa'a gwahee'
            I am going
    4. gahidọhọ ageegεne'   huiwe'hee ne' gaenọ'
            yeidos   I see it walking   the song
    5. gahidọhọ ageegεne'   huiwe'hee   hewageenọ'
            yeidos   I see it walking   I went there
    6. yowine   ga'ayaha :]
            (3 times and repeat)
    7. yowine ga'âyo'o'o' yoho'o'oh   he'e hee hoji'ha hawine hayoo . . .
    8. yowine . . . .   jodaha hawine . . .
    9. yoho johε nọga   dadiyọ yoho   (repeat)
            Yonder song they come in
    10. yoho jọgwayọ yoho . . .
            we came
    11. ogεsεn ogεs sεhε'n   hoganọhsayεndadye' yowine
            They're stomping, stomping the whole length of the longhouse
            (Arise)
    12. doodi dodi dwadεnọgehεhät
            We will try
            (Standing)
    13. oh'dεjọ ha'a'a oh'dεjọ ne'ho nage'εnọ haide   gwa' gwa hee'
            It is going here, my song
    14. o'jọgwanọ sohiidε' hai he . . .
            We the house fill with noise of stomping
    15. ohdεjọ :] ne'ho o'jọgwaya'dεdεso' :] gwa . . .
            It's going: here we turning our bodies side to side. We are stirring
            (Pretend to dance.)
    16. ohdεjọ :] o'jọgwagohsεdọsọ' :]
            It is going: we turn our faces side to side. We peer about.

17. ohdɛjǫ :] ohdɛnjǫhǫ' :]
    It is going, moving, it has started. (Start to dance.)
    (Dancing)
18. gwa' gwahee' wɛ'ɛniyo hɛhɛ :] gwa' gwahe'
19. gwa' gwahee' ha'eniyo hɛhɛ :] hainiyo hɛhɛ :] gwa . . .
20. gwa' gwahee' gwɛ' niyo hɛhɛ :] gweniyo hɛhɛ :] gwa . . .
21. wɛɛniyo . . .
22. ha'awiyo hɛhɛ haiwiyo . . .
23. ha'ehiyo . . . haehiyo . . .
24. hogayaa hogayaa ha'a deyǫgwahɛ hɛnɛgohdǫ'ǫ] hogayaa . . .
    We have fulfilled the songs
25. hogaya hogaya ha'a dejǫgwahɛ' nǫgesgwɛ hogaya . . .
    We have repeated the songs
26. dejǫgwadǫhɛ' jǫgohdǫ'ǫ hogaya . . .
    We passed through narrow valleys
27. hogaya' . . . gwa'gwa he wahaa'a :] nehi otadiya'a dodadiye'isǫ'ǫ
    (Dancers stagger)   All their bodies are swaying
28. sa'yodɛ'ɛ sayo'ǫdǫǫ haihe haihe :] hai he gwa . . .
    Woman you are lucky, you will recover
29. watcǫcǫ watcǫdǫ haihe :]
30. i'gɛnde'e i'gɛnde'e hi hi wa'agonǫnhonkdɛ'
    I know why she did get sick
31. wa'khejɛ'h wa'khejɛhɛ'ɛ i'gɛnde'e ho'dajeshǫ'ǫ
    I make her will, I cure her   I know
32. hayǫ'wa :] yohigeegɛ yowigeegɛ : hɛɛ'
33. ha'yowǫǫ :] hai'ge'gɛ haiheh haihe :]
34. hojigɛgɛ hojigɛgɛh' jigɛ gɛ'ɛhɛ :]
35. ho' gainondiyǫdǫ nǫgwainǫ ha'yowe higɛ'ne hayǫwe ha'yowani
    Song is mixed,   our songs are confused
36. hogahɛnodiyǫndɛɛ' nogwa'henǫ'gɛ' ǫhǫǫ
    The songs are clashing, our songs
37. yowihi :] gahidaniyondǫ'hǫǫ :]
    The yeidos is hung up overhead
38. yo'owihi :] neyo'owine hɛ'ɛɛgahidaniyondǫ'hǫ
39. yo'ohoo ganesagǫ ne' ho we'ey'ho :]
    beneath the hillside   they are walking
40. jihǫd'odɛ :] gadogɛ :]
    They stand up a twig at a certain place (by magic)

41. jiho . . . gano'sɛganǫhshɛhe' :]

     They erect a twig in the middle of the lodge (stand rattles on end.)

42. jiho . . . ehda'geha hahǫdɛhǫwihi :]

     They erect the twig low down he is carrying it (place rattle on floor)

43. wa'khenyodɛ' :] gadoogɛ :]

     I stood her up in a certain place

44. wa'k henyodɛ' ganǫhshɛ :]

     I stood her up in the center of the lodge

45. wa'ha'a :] nehe keyadɛnǫhgeahdǫ :]

     I will try to have her dance →

46. do'odi do'odihi' keyahdɛdjedohǫ :]

     I make her go (She, the sponsor, starts dancing)

47. ho'tgainǫgǫ'daje' hot . . . .

     The last song (for the company). (Masker goes out to get mask)
     (Masker)

48. hojigɛgɛh hojigɛgɛhɛ dehadigǫhsahe'ah :]

     The two masks look in →

49. hojigɛgɛh . . . dehanoyay'ɛndonehe

     They are coming dancing

50. ojistagweniyǫdǫhǫ wa'ahee :] nehe "] wahe

     Embers are ready she says

51. ojistagweni deyoditha' :] 'a hɛnǫdonyǫhǫ' hǫ'ǫ'ǫ

     Embers are ready they two say to each other, they all are saying

52. hai hee he'i . . . deyadigǫsa'negɛ :]

     (Mask and man) Their two faces are against each other

53. hai he . . . deyagigohsa'ne gɛ :]

     Our two faces are vis-`a-vis

54. hai . . . dehigǫhsanegɛ :]

     Their two faces are together (Mask blows on man)

55. onɛ'yai :] hai he

     fire (red hot rocks)

56. hai . . . (solo); hai he he'i (chorus) o'dagwɛ ho'dagwɛ :]

     ashes flying about

57. hai . . . (helper) hai (solo) wačisdayanǫdanǫ (S) hai hei (Ch)

     Sparks are streaking

58. ha'tgǫhsayanǫdanǫ (S) hai he (Ch)

     He is peering around turning his face from side to side

59. hai he hei (S and Ch) họ'ọ'ọ' (Mask) odiwahęnọwehęnt gahidọ'
    ọgowaha'a

>   Let us put the songs overhead of the great i'dos (sharp point)

60. hai họ'ọ'ọ odidwahęnọwehęnt gayoweo'ọ'gowaha'a

>   Let us put away the songs overhead of the great sharp point

61. hai he hei . . . onęsawahdęndi'a'a   hai . . . nọgwaenọ(geọ')

>   Now he has departed   Our songs that are past (dead)

>   hai . . . gahidohọgowaha'a   gwa he . . .

>   of the Great yeidos

62. hai . . . onę sawahdęndi'a   hai . . . . gahidohdoowa'a

>   Now it has gone home   the great yeidos ceremony

63. hai . . . gayowo'ọgoowa'a   hai . . . dewanọvayęhdọ'nee's

>   the great sharp point (mask)   it is peering around

64. yohaha hei :] deganọgeoda' dyesọ   [: gwa gwahe :] neeto

>   The horned ones are butting each other

>   (Dancers bow and put their rattles up to their heads and butt each other.)

Shamans   Hadii 'dos   C.J. John, 1941

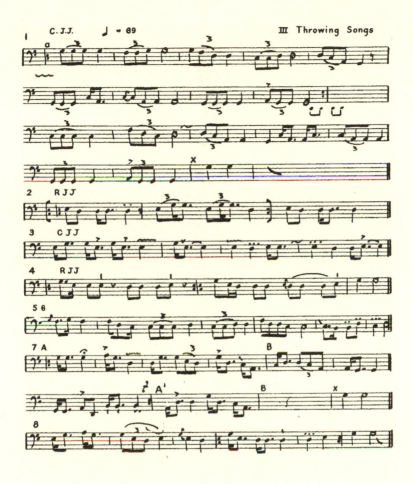

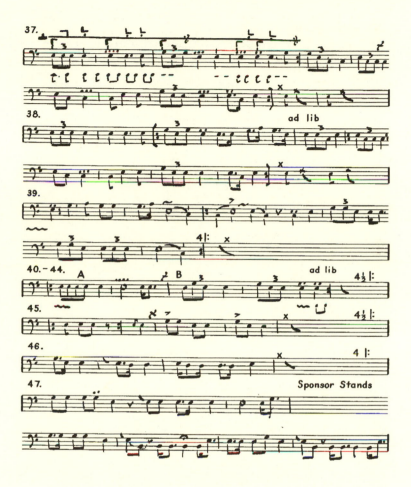

APPENDIX C

The Society of the Medicine Men at Six Nations

Hadihi:ʔdu:s, as the Onondagas at Six Nations on the Grand River call singing the celebration songs of the Medicine Men's Society, is one of the most exciting of Iroquois ceremonies. The songs of twelve to fifteen men shaking gourd rattles in unison fill the narrow confines of a log house to overflowing, and in the overtones one hears the cries of mystic animals that were the familiars of past generations of shamans. The rites are more or less secret, and singing the songs outside the medicine lodge is said by some adherents to bring illness or accidents to the singer who ignores the taboo.[1]

Alexander Goldenweiser participated in the rite during his fieldwork in 1912 for the Anthropological Survey of Canada. He recorded its songs on wax cylinders, but they have been lost. The singer then, as in 1941 when I recorded the songs (Fenton 1942a, 1942b), was Chief Joseph Logan (Thadada:hoʔ), who, out of consideration of my knowing the ceremony among the Senecas and the fact that his previous recording had vanished, desired to put down the Onondaga version

---

1. After the program notes that accompanied the recording *Songs from the Iroquois Longhouse* (Fenton 1942a, 1942b).

of the rite for future generations of his own people and for scientific study. The recordings have recently been made available to his successors, who, having lost parts of the ritual, wanted to restore the ceremony for the people of Six Nations.

Chief Logan learned the songs from John Echo, a famous singer at Six Nations on Grand River at the turn of the past century, and from old Dave Skye. In the 1940s Chief Logan was the leading singer of the ritual. In recording, he remembered the songs by recalling the sequence of key words, which he denominated at the same time on his fingers, doubling a finger as he recalled the name of a song. He preferred to sing them piecemeal, recording a strip or two at a time, lest he omit anything. He thought there should be fifty songs in all, but we came out with forty-five.

The history of the medicine society is shrouded in antiquity. Chief Logan's account of its descent from an ancient society of shamans suggests the Huron Awataerrohi, whose members specialized in handling fire, particularly hot stones, and the Atirenda society, whose members pretended to kill one another with charms (Trigger 1976: 80). Chief Logan told me:

> In the old times, perhaps a thousand years ago, men of each Iroquois nation had these songs for contesting magic power. Only magicians belonged to this society, and only magicians danced. Their songs referred to their powers. While dancing, they demonstrated their powers by "throwing" or "shooting" sharp objects such as "horns" [antler], which activity gave the name of "sharp point" (*gaiʔdonʔ*) to one part of the ritual. Or one shaman would sing, "Something [like a bear] is running around." The magician would transform himself into a bear and run around there in the lodge. Another shaman would cause a twig to stand of itself in the center of the room while the other medicine men danced around it. Still another in turn would go to the fire, remove red-hot stones, and juggle them. A man lacking this kind of power could not do this.
>
> Later, people decided to abandon such songs. But the old songs kept continually molesting the people, who felt com-

pelled to do something about it. The old magicians held council. They decided that they could not abandon the songs, and that they must carry on. They have continued through all of the generations that followed. Now only the songs have power. Now only the one who wears the mask has the power to handle live embers when he impersonates the ancients. No one any longer tosses hot rocks.

As among the Senecas, members of the Six Nations medicine society have dreamed of the songs or have been cured by the ceremony. And the same moiety arrangements obtain. Invitation is by kernels of corn. An invited member who becomes ill and cannot attend must burn tobacco in his own fire and explain his absence to the animal familiars. The meetings follow the Seneca format:

1. Greetings, thanks, and announcements
2. Tobacco invocation to the tutelaries
3. A period of throwing songs
4. Beginning songs before medicine dance
5. The medicine dance (*ganonyahgwen?*)

The published record album presents samples of each style of song. Throwing songs appeal to the power of song to help the sponsor of the feast. This style, by the opposite moiety of singers performing individually, precedes the main event. A second song has only nonsense vocables. The third member's song speaks to the supernatural powers of the raccoon:

> He's a witch, that raccoon.
> I never knew that the raccoon has supernatural power.

A fourth member sings, with variations:

> Wolf runs on the open fields,
> He runs in the wide valleys,
> He runs on the ridges, etc.

The running wolf theme is a favorite in Iroquois song style. It occurs in the songs to renew the Little Water medicine and in the Great Feather Dance.

Beginning songs. The song leader sings four introductory songs, either before the period of throwing songs or to preface the medicine dance. This preface is called "Going to the end of the song." The leader says, "So now indeed it is up to you to sing the medicine dance. And moreover, our song shall commence from the beginning and go on to the very last song" (there shall be no interruptions). A sample song speaks to the people:

> All of my grandchildren's houses
> Are stretched out in a long line.

The medicine speaks to the people, whom the medicine has as grandchildren.

Medicine dance. The main act of the ceremony is the round dance, the so-called medicine dance, or *ganonyahgwen?*. The singers remain seated for the first seventeen songs. Halfway through the eighteenth song, they stand and sing before the benches, and at the twentieth song, the dance commences. The songs run in pairs. For example:

1. The bugs (larvae) are conversing.
2. The Great White Owls are conversing.

The two creatures are familiars of the medicine society. They hear the songs afar and discuss them. Soon, Chief Logan explained, they will realize that they are invited to attend, and they will come to the lodge. In the singing style, the dual form of the verb "to talk" is split between the first and second lines of the meter.

Skipping to the nineteenth song, the animal familiars of the shamans having arrived, the melody changes and the round dance begins. The dancers start at the twentieth song with the cue, "Sharp point is moving." At song 35, a shaman confesses:

I threw it; I threw it;
It lodged in my own mouth.
I threw it; I threw it.

"Sharp point" (*gahi:ʔdohonʔ*) is an obscure archaic word from which the ceremony takes its name. A dart thrown by one of the magicians has lodged in his own mouth. Perhaps one of the other magicians has turned it back on him.

I will not reiterate the intervening songs, particularly those that relate to the masker, his entrance, his marshalling of dancers, handling fire, and treatment of patients, but will skip to the final two songs—44 and 45—that Chief Logan recorded:

Now, now,
The ceremony is gone through.

Now, now, it is finished.
Now, now, the steam of our cooking
Has cooled, you medicine men [shamans].

I long suspected that the *hanaʔhi:ʔdo:s* celebrated by the Six Nations on Grand River had been influenced by the *medewiwin,* or Grand Medicine Lodge, of the upper Great Lakes Central Algonquians. I was unable to establish the connection, however, until direct historic evidence appeared in the research of Ruth B. Phillips, who graciously granted me permission to quote from her published report (1984: 35–36). As Phillips recounts, Edward Walsh (1766–1832), surgeon of the Forty-ninth Regiment of Foot, went among the Indians resident on the Grand River to vaccinate them for smallpox, a scourge still dreaded in the summer of 1804. Just then the Mississaugas (eastern Ojibwas) and upper Cayugas lived as close neighbors near the present city of Brantford, Ontario. Walsh was invited to witness a performance of the *mide* conducted by a visiting Miami shaman, and his account demonstrates an unusual talent for ethnography.

His hosts not only built him a pole and bark wigwam and feasted him with meat, fish, and game birds but also offered to admit him as a member of their company of shamans. As in the Iroquois case, he wrote: "Initiates are at the same time priests, prophets, physicians, and jugglers, and like all of these who know more than the multitude they exercise almost absolute sway in the respective tribes."

Walsh said he witnessed the initiation of a young man who for some time had been probationary. In his own words:

> I was witness in part to the initiation of a young man who had been disciplined for some time previous in a state of probation. A dog was first sacrificed and eaten by the priests—the bone scraped and wrapped in the skin. Before the lodge of the chief there was a small arched hut erected. It was very close and barely high enough for a person to sit up. The Candidate sat before the entrance naked, his arms fastened to his sides with strips of birch bark and his body oiled and painted. All being now prepared the most extraordinary figure that ever was formed among the demons of theatre strode out of his wigwam. He was a Miami chief, gaunt and big boned and more than six feet high. His features were terrific, tho' not ugly. Projecting brows overhung a pair of small keen black eyes, the nose large and triangular, the visage lengthy, the chin square with a bushy beard, and the mouth as the phrase is extending from ear to ear. A white line divided the features into two equal parts, the right side was painted red with vermillion, the left black. His conjuring cap which he afterwards presented to me was made of the shaggy skin of a buffalo's forehead with the ears and horns on. A buffalo robe hung on his broad shoulders the inside of which was worked in figures of sun, moon, and stars and other hieroglyphics.
>
> he addressed the young [man] in a short speech uttered with the deepest intonation as from the bottom of his breast. He then threw a pebble at him pretty forcibly. The young Indian the instant he was hit fell back and appeared to be in a swoon. Two other Jugglers with capuchin skins over their heads thrust him in the state of insensibility into the hut which

had been previously heated with hot stones upon which water had been thrown and a hot vapour raised. Meanwhile the hierarch threw himself on the ground, muttering words as if he was talking to somebody and rolling himself from side to side and working like a person in strong convulsions. In this state he was dragged into his wigwam and left there to dream.

In about half an hour he sallied forth and made a sign to his assistants up[on] which they drew out by the heels the miserable candidate from the oven. He was bathed in a clammy sweat and had all the appearance of a recent corpse—no perceptible breath or pulse. Our hierarch no[t] very discomposed stooped over him and uttered aloud his incantations. His two assistants sat at either side, each with a skin pouch in which was some ignited substance that smoked which they kept puffing into his ears. In a few minutes [he] fetched a deep sigh and opened his eyes upon which all the spectators shewed the strongest signs of approbation crying out as in chorus "hogh, hogh, hogh." Only principal warriors were admitted to this curious scene and I by special favour made one in the circle.

Glossary

daennonhgwaʔthaʔ. He raises up the songs (song leader).

dekniwadonta:ʔ. Second period (group of songs).

Donishohgwageh:wenʔ. Name of Good Hunter.

dyogohsa:t; dyojenʔdahgon. First period (group of songs).

ʔeti:so:t ; sedwaso:t. Grandmother (moon); our grandparent; ego to
    medicine.

gaenonʔwetahon. Inserted songs (intermezzo).

gaʔgawisheʔ. Paddle, spatula.

ga:ʔgendaʔ. Flute or whistle.

gagonhsaʔ. Mask, False Face, masker.

gahgaʔgo:wa:ʔ. Raven, Big Crow, messenger.

gahi:ʔdonʔ,-gowa:ʔ (= *yei:ʔdo:s*), *gayoweonʔgo:wa.* Sharp Point, Great
    Sharp Point, "Pumpkin Shake."

ganenyonʔdonʔ. Accepting the kernel of corn (invitation).

gano:daʔ. Night song.

ganonhse:s. Longhouse.

ganonyahgwenʔ or *ganonyahgwenʔgo:wa.* The Great Medicine Dance,
    or round dance.

ganonyahgwenʔ gaenonʔ. Medicine dance song.

ganon:yonk. Thanksgiving speech.

gasak?hneh. "When I cough" (November).

gende?onkhneh. Moon of Green Corn.

geonkhneh. Harvest moon.

go?negonhjeta?. Water spreading songs.

hade:ne:t. Bundle holder, keeper.

hadihadi:ya?s, gahadi:ya?gon. Going through the forest.

hadiyen?gwa?ye:ni; ?ondiyen?gwa?yeons; hadino:daiyai?. "Putting
    tobacco down," renewal.

hadyaswas. Messenger.

hahoanonsta:s, ongwahashe?. Doorkeeper, helper, our servant.

haneyon:? (m.), *yeneyon:?* (f.), *da:ya?dowewetha?.* Clairvoyant.

hasteistha?. Conductor.

heyennonga:dasta?. Fourth period (group of songs).

hodiyenonyen:don goenondyetha?. They have personal songs for throwing.

honiyonsko:t. He (sponsor) prepared the sweat lodge.

hotcinohgen?. A male member of the medicine society; bundle
    holder.

hotes, hotesyon:ni:h, godenshon? (f.). Patient, sponsor ("he has the cer-
    emony cooking").

howondiyahswaye:ni. They pick as crows on carrion.

i:?do:s or *hadi:?do:s, yei?do:s.* Celebration rite of the medicine com-
    pany.

ko:weh (three times). Scalp cry (death).

Neh HO-NOH-TCI-NOH-GAH. The Guardians of the Little
    Waters (Arthur C. Parker).

Neh honontcinohgen?. The Medicine-Holders' Society, medicine
    company, society, members.

niga:nega?ah. Little Water (Society).

niga:nega?a:h dwahso:t. A little water, our grandparent.

n:iskowakhneh , jis-. Midwinter, "longer days" (January–February).

?odenoga:de?. Third period (group of songs).

oennonsha:ye ; o?nyaysnha:yen?. Slow song tempo, adagio; slow stick.

oennui?ah. "Deranged," "hot," or curing songs.

oenonssno:we? ; o?hnyasnno:wa. Faster tempo; fast stick.

ʔohsadaʔge:aʔ. Dew Eagle.

ʔoi:yenʔ. Swamp saxifrage (*Saxifragia pennsylvanica* L.).

oniyenskwadaiyenʔgo:wa. The great hot ceremony.

o:nyaʔsaʔ gastawenʔshaʔ. Squash or gourd rattle.

otadongwahgwa:t. To kindle the flame, raise up the song.

ʔotgwanonyonʔ dwaso:t. I return thanks to our grandfathers.

ʔotgwanonyonʔ swatcinonhgenʔshonʔ. "I return thanks (greet) you
    (familiars) of the medicine society."

ʔo:ya:giʔ. Berry juice.

ʔoyaikneh. Berry Moon.

ʔoyenʔgwaʔon:weh. Indian tobacco (*Nicotiana rustica* L.).

sawonnonʔtga:ʔ, ensa:wenonʔtga:ʔ, ʔeondiʔdonh. Ceremony of release at
    end of confinement.

tha:yo:nih. Wolf.

wadizeonwen: gadzeot. Putting the song over the fire.

wainondehnoʔya:k. Throwing songs at each other.

wayonʔento gaenonʔ. He has spilled the songs (the conductor).

wenniyonsko:t. Sweat lodge.

wondiyiennondiʔ. Throwing a song.

yohowenʔ. Brant.

Bibliography

Barbeau, C. Marius. 1915. *Huron and Wyandot Mythology.* Anthropological Series II, Memoirs of the Canadian Geological Survey 80, Ottawa.

Beauchamp, William M. 1901. "The Good Hunter and the Iroquois Medicine." *Journal of American Folklore* 54: 153–59.

Chafe, Wallace L. 1961. *Seneca Thanksgiving Rituals.* Bureau of American Ethnology Bulletin 183. Washington, D.C.: Smithsonian Institution.

————. 1963. *Handbook of the Seneca Language.* New York State Museum and Science Service Bulletin 388. Albany.

Clarke, Peter D. 1870. *Origin and Traditional History of the Wyandotte.* Toronto: Hunter Rose and Company.

Congdon, Charles E. 1967. *The Allegany Oxbow.* Little Valley, N.Y.

Converse, Harriett Maxwell. 1908. *Myths and Legends of the New York State Iroquois.* Edited by Arthur C. Parker. New York State Museum Bulletin 125. Albany.

Cornplanter, Jesse J. 1938. *Legends of the Longhouse.* Philadelphia: J. B. Lippincott.

Curtin, Jeremiah, and J. N. B. Hewitt. 1918. "Seneca Fiction, Legends, and Myths." *Thirty-second Annual Report of the Bureau of*

American Ethnology for theYears 1910–11, pp. 37–813.
Washington, D.C.: Smithsonian Institution.

Doty, Lockwood L. 1876. *History of Livingston County, NewYork.*
Geneseo, N.Y.: Edward E. Doty.

Fenton,William N. 1934–46. Field Notes: Allegany, Cattaraugus,
Tonawanda, and Six Nations. Fenton Papers, American
Philosophical Society Library. Philadelphia.

————. 1936. *An Outline of Seneca Ceremonies at Coldspring
Longhouse.*Yale University Publications in Anthropology 9. New
Haven, Conn.

————, recorder and editor. 1942a. *Songs from the Iroquois
Longhouse.* Folk Music of the United States. Archive of
Folksong, Album 6.Washington, D.C.: Library of Congress.

————. 1942b. *Songs from the Iroquois Longhouse: Program Notes for
an Album of American Indian Music from the EasternWoodlands.*
Washington, D.C.: Smithsonian Institution Publication 3691.

————. 1978. "'AboriginallyYours,' Jesse J. Cornplanter, Ha-
Yonh-Wonh-Ish, the Snipe (Seneca) (1889–1957)." In *American
Indian Intellectuals,* edited by Margot Liberty, pp. 177–95.
Proceedings of the American Ethnological Society.

————. 1979. "The Great Good Medicine." *NewYork State Journal of
Medicine* 79 (10): 1603–9.

————. 1980. "Tobacco Invocation: Seneca. William Fenton and
Henry Redeye. Edited byWallace Chafe." In *Northern Iroquoian
Texts,* edited by Marianne Mithun and HanniWoodbury, pp.
3–8. IJAL-NATS Monograph 4. Chicago: University of
Chicago Press.

————. 1987. *The False Faces of the Iroquois.* Norman: University of
Oklahoma Press.

————.1998. *The Great Law and the Longhouse:A Political History of
the Iroquois Confederacy.* Norman: University of Oklahoma Press.

————.1991.*The Iroquois Eagle Dance:An Offshoot of the Calumet
Dance.*With a new introduction byWilliam N. Fenton. Reprint
of 1953 BAE Bulletin156, 1953.

Fenton,William N., and Merle H. Deardorff. 1943. "The Last

Passenger Pigeon Hunts of the Cornplanter Senecas." *Journal of the Washington Academy of Sciences* 33 (10): 289–315.

Goldenweiser, Alexander A. 1922. *Early Civilization.* New York: Alfred Knopf.

Jacket, John. 1849. Text of *Gano:da,* the All-Night Chant of the Little Water Society. Manuscript. Huntington Free Library and Reading Room, Bronx, N.Y.

Johnson, Elias (Tuscarora). 1881. *Legends, Traditions, and Laws of the Six Nations.* Lockport, N.Y.: Union Printing and Publishing Company.

Keppler, J. 1941. "Comments on Certain Iroquois Masks." *Contributions from the Museum of the American Indian—Heye Foundation* 12 (4): 1–40.

Kurath, Gertrude P. 1964. *Iroquois Music and Dance: Ceremonial Arts of Two Seneca Longhouses.* Bureau of American Ethnology Bulletin 187. Washington, D.C.: Smithsonian Institution.

Lafitau, Father Joseph-François. 1974 [1724]. *Customs of the American Indians Compared with the Customs of Primitive Times,* vol. 1. Edited and translated by W. N. Fenton and Elizabeth L. Moore. Toronto: Champlain Society.

———. 1977 [1724]. *Customs of the American Indians Compared with the Customs of Primitive Times,* vol. 2. Edited and translated by W. N. Fenton and Elizabeth L. Moore. Toronto: Champlain Society.

Loeb, Edwin M. 1929. *Tribal Initiations and Secret Societies.* University of California Publications in American Archaeology and Ethnology. Berkeley.

Myrtle, Minnie (pseudonym of Anna Cummings Johnson Miller). 1885. *The Iroquois, or the Bright Side of Indian Character.* New York: D. Appleton.

Parker, Arthur C. 1908. "Neh Ho-non-tci-noh-geh: The Guardians of the Little Waters, a Seneca Medicine Society." In *Myths and Legends of the New York State Iroquois,* by Harriett Maxwell Converse, edited by Arthur C. Parker, pp. 149–70. New York State Museum Bulletin 125. Albany.

————. 1909. "Secret Medicine Societies of the Seneca." *American Anthropologist* (n.s.) 2 (2): 161–85.

Phillips, Ruth B. 1984. *Patterns of Power: The Jasper Grant Collection and Great Lakes Indian Art of the Early Nineteenth Century.* Kleinburg, Ont.: McMichael Canadian Collection.

Radin, Paul. 1916. "The Winnebago Tribe." *Thirty-seventh Annual Report of the Bureau of American Ethnology,* pp. 33–550. Washington, D.C.: Smithsonian Institution.

Rothenberg, Jerome, ed. 1972. *Shaking the Pumpkin: Traditional Poetry of the Indian North Americas.* Garden City, N.Y.: Doubleday.

Shimony, Annemarie. 1961a. *Conservatism among the Iroquois at the Six Nations Reserve.* Yale University Publications in Anthropology 65. New Haven, Conn. (Reprint with new introduction, 1994, Syracuse University Press.)

————. 1961b. "The Iroquois Fortune Tellers and Their Conservative Influence." In *Symposium on Cherokee and Iroquois Culture,* edited by W. N. Fenton and John Gulick, pp. 205–11. Bureau of American Ethnology Bulletin 180: 205–211. Washington, D.C.: Smithsonian Institution.

————. 1970. "Iroquois Witchcraft at Six Nations." In *Systems of North American Witchcraft and Sorcery,* edited by Deward E. Walker, Jr., pp. 239–65. Anthropological Monographs of the University of Idaho. Moscow, Idaho.

Thwaites, Reuben Gold, ed. 1896–1901. *The Jesuit Relations and Allied Documents: Travels and Explorations of the Jesuit Missionaries in New France, 1610–1791.* 73 vols. Cleveland: Burrows Brothers. Reprint, New York: Pageant Press, 1959.

Trigger, Bruce G. 1976. *The Children of Ataentsic: A History of the Huron People to 1660.* 2 vols. Montreal: McGill University Press.

Wallace, Anthony F. C. 1958. "Dreams and the Wishes of the Soul: A Type of Psychoanalytical Theory among the Seventeenth-Century Iroquois." *American Anthropologist* 60 (2): 234–48.

Wilson, Edmund. 1959. *Apologies to the Iroquois.* New York: Farrar, Straus, and Giroux.

Index